HOLLYWOOD LOLITAS

The Nymphet Syndrome in the Movies

Marianne Sinclair

An Owl Book
Henry Holt and Company
New York

Published by Henry Holt and Company, Inc.,
115 West 18th Street, New York, New York 10011.

Library of Congress Cataloging-in-Publication Data
Sinclair, Marianne, 1940–
Hollywood Lolitas.
1. Sex in motion pictures.   2. Nabokov, Vladimir
Vladimirovich, 1899–1977.   Lolita.   3. Nabokov, Vladimir
Vladimirovich, 1899–1977—Influence.   I. Title.
II. Title: Nymphet syndrome in the movies.
PN1995.9.S45S55   1988   791.43'09'09353   88-21604
ISBN 0-8050-0931-0 (A Owl Book: pbk.)

Henry Holt books are available at special discounts for bulk
purchases for sales promotions, premiums, fund raising, or
educational use. Special editions or book excerpts can also be
created to specification.

        For details, contact:

        Special Sales Director
        Henry Holt and Company, Inc.
        115 West 18th Street
        New York, New York 10011

First American Edition

Designed by Ken Kitchen
Printed in the United States of America
10   9   8   7   6   5   4   3   2   1

Excerpts from Lolita copyright © 1955 by Vladimir Nabokov;
by special arrangement with the Estate of Vladimir Nabokov.

We would like to thank the following for the use of
photographs from their archives and for their help in
researching visual materials: the John Kobal Collection, the
National Film Archive, Herve Tardy at the Gamma Photo
Agency, Paris, and Tony Gale at Pictorial Press. We would also
like to thank the film companies responsible for many of the
artists in the book: Paramount Films, Columbia Pictures,
Warner Brothers, Universal Pictures, United Artists Films, 20th
Century-Fox and MGM Films. Every effort has been made to
reach copyright holders or their representatives. The pub-
lishers will be pleased to correct omissions or mistakes in
future editions.

CONTENTS

1. Celluloid Nymphet

'Irving Thalberg used to tell me: "When you write a love scene, think of your heroine as a little puppy dog, cuddling up to her master, wagging an imaginary tail, and gazing up at him as if he were God." '

Anita Loos (*Kiss Hollywood Goodbye*)

When Vladimir Nabokov's novel, *Lolita*, was first published in 1955, it caused a sensation. It defined a myth: the nymphet. The nymphet had existed before *Lolita*, of course, as the novel's unhappy erudite anti-hero Humbert Humbert was the first to point out, but she had not yet been defined. She had not been identified, classified as a *genre*, as a literary, cultural, cinematic and sociological phenomenon, so instantly recognizable that Lolita came to life retrospectively as well as by anticipation.

Nabokov's definition of the prototype was somewhat restricted: 'Between the age limits of nine and fourteen there occur maidens who, to certain bewitched travellers, twice or many times older than they, reveal their true nature which is not human, but nymphic (that is, demoniac); and these chosen creatures I propose to designate as "nymphets".'

But the term 'Lolita', which instantly became a reference point in Western culture, soon came to cover a much wider age-group than nine to fourteen. People can refer to a six or to a twenty-six-year-old as 'the Lolita type', and everyone understands what is meant. In a child, it suggests a feminine coquettishness and a hint of sensuality well beyond one's years. In a grown woman, it hints at a childish coyness, an immaturity of both character and appearance. For example, Tatum O'Neal and Mary Pickford were both nymphet types when their respective ages were nine and twenty-nine. The two ends of the age-spectrum have in common a capacity to arouse the Humbert Humbert that lies barely dormant in many men, a capacity for 'innocent' provocation and seduction that might be called 'Lolitaesque' or 'Lolita-ish'.

In Nabokov's novel, the besotted Humbert Humbert actually becomes the nymphet's lover almost half-way through the book, through a highly improbable series of propitious circumstances that brought them together. Yet Nabokov-Humbert was very keen to specify the real danger of Lolita's appeal: 'I am not concerned with so-called "sex" at all. Anybody can imagine those elements of animality. A greater endeavour lures me on: to fix once and for all the perilous magic of nymphets.' To each Humbert his Lolita: from the chaste girl-worshipper to the child rapist, the variety of nuances is infinite, though certain aspects of both extremes can merge confusingly; Nabokov spoke of 'the portion of hell and the portion of heaven in that strange, awful, maddening world – nymphet love. The beastly and beautiful merged at one point, and it is that borderline I would like to fix.'

Humbert Humbert's passion for Lolita contained varying shades of feeling and emotion: he desired her, yet also desired to protect her innocence from his desire. He was her legal step-father and genuinely loved her as a daughter, yet it was also his own boyhood and first adolescent love that he relived and sought to recapture. In the beginning, he loved her almost chastely and certainly hopelessly, since there seemed no prospect of ever getting her. But then she became his mistress and he loved her sexually, jealously, possessively, as a man can love a woman of whatever age. Finally, Lolita ran away, leaving him for another. By the time he found her again, she had grown

up, lost her looks, was bespectacled and heavily pregnant. And still he loved her, enough to beg her to come back to him and, enough to commit murder because of her. The cinema is a natural idiom for illustrating the magic of the Lolita myth. From its inception, it has been rich in nymphets who eluded or gave in to Humbert Humberts of all shapes and sizes. The movie is Lolita's element, her medium. When Nabokov's Lolita saved up to run away from the gilded cage in which her step-father kept her locked up, she dreamed of going to Hollywood, like so many other, real-life girls. If Lolita had made it to Hollywood, she would have met a lot of other Humbert Humberts, mature older men ready to help and/or take advantage of the nymphet's innate narcissistic drive. In the eighty-year-long history of Hollywood, its young girls have been referred to as aspiring actresses, starlets, baby harlots, cheap cuties, dolls, or fully-fledged stars with their own dressing-rooms and million-dollar contracts at an age when they still had to be lifted onto a studio-chair. Some of them were ready for anything to get into pictures; others were irreproachably chaste; others still were reluctant to sell their charms for a chance to act in a movie. Yet isn't becoming a movie actress all about trying to 'sell' one's looks and sex-appeal on a screen in the first place? The nymphet has an innate narcissistic drive, and the way to gratify it is by appearing on the big screen.

Hollywood Humbert Humbert was lurking in wait for Hollywood Lolita, both on screen and off. Some men are just more Humbertish than others. They take what they can get in the way of women and girls, but the younger the girls the better. 'It was Eve he lay with, but it was Lilith he sighed after,' explains Nabokov's Humbert, who bedded Lolita's mother while longing for the daughter. It is a case of arrested development, not in the girl but in the man: Nabokov opens *Lolita* with a long description of how Humbert, when a 'faunlet' of thirteen, loved and lost a little girl of his own age. Some men overcome that nostalgia for their first *grand amour*, others do not.

Left: *Thirties moviegoers loved to see their budding nymphets dressing up as grown-up jazz babies.* Below: *Four-year-old curls and coy bare shoulders ape the vampish poses of the Ziegfield years.*

The boys of twelve or fourteen who fall madly in love with a nymphet are not yet Humberts. It is only when they cannot outgrow their youthful infatuations, when they go on trying to relive it throughout their lives, that one can talk of a 'nymphet syndrome'. Typically, the mature Humbert remains a quivering boy at heart, unable to move on to the next stage, to love a woman his own age. It is not surprising that so many flock to the cinema to see the shadow of a vanished childhood sweetheart on the screen. And, as we shall see, grown women too vicariously relive the days of their Lolita power.

It is usually no more than a sentimental longing, and therefore harmless. Nabokov's Humbert was a pathological case insofar as he longed for sexual possession of his pre-teen love-object. But then, in a sense, Lolita too was a pathological case: at twelve, she was ready to accept the advances of a middle-aged male. In fact, it was she who seduced Humbert, technically speaking, out of curiosity, 'just for fun'. Subsequently, aged only fourteen, she fell in love with another middle-aged man, a famous play-wright who had already helped her to get a part in a play. The fact that she was fatherless may have had something to do with it, but it is also true that a lot of very young girls are prepared, like their older sisters, to accept and even encourage the advances of older men in a position of power. This has been especially true of Hollywood, which is all about sex and power and making deals between the two. The casting couch is not a recent invention: Mack Sennett was accused

of making generous use of it, and some of his budding bathing beauties were barely into their teens.

Hollywood's Humberts usually got away with their Lolita complex, but there could sometimes be all hell to pay. Some of Hollywood's most notorious scandals, spanning fifty years of movie history, involved an older man and a *bona fide* nymphet. Charlie Chaplin, Errol Flynn and Roman Polanski all faced prosecution for sexual activity with minors. Each case contains elements to be found in the novel of *Lolita*. Like Nabokov's Humbert Humbert, Chaplin and Polanski were both cultured Europeans (synonymous with decadence in American eyes) accused by an irate US public opinion of having corrupted an innocent all-American girl (in some cases more than one). Even Flynn was non-American (he was born in Tasmania). All of them were to protest, like Humbert, that it was they who had been seduced. And, as in *Lolita*, there was a third figure who played a significant role in the whole affair: Lolita's mother.

No nymphet is complete without her mother, especially in the case of Hollywood Lolita: 'The wayward child, the egoistic mother, the panting maniac – these are not only vivid characters in a unique story; they warn us of dangerous trends; they point out potent evils,' Nabokov wrote. The original Lolita's mother fell in love with Humbert Humbert, married him and thus unintentionally brought about the situation whereby Humbert had access to her daughter. Hollywood Lolita's mother is more knowing, more calculating. She usually stands at arm's length from potential Humberts herself, but she knows what her little darling is worth down to the last cent, and she means to make sure that the film world's Humberts pay the full price. Nine times out of ten, she has been living off her baby as a child model during the pre-nymphet years. The child-star's mother is as notorious off-screen as her baby may be famous on-screen. She is often a ripe and rampant predator, looking after her daughter's interests, as only *she* construes them to be.

Hollywood Lolita's mother figured prominently in the court cases. The men involved were themselves victims of the casting-couch syndrome, eager and willing victims perhaps, but still victims. For the mothers of the Lolitas involved went all out to exploit the sexual interest their daughters had aroused in famous, powerful, wealthy men. Lilita McMurray, Chaplin's child-bride (her name must have influenced Nabokov) and Polanski's 'Sandra' (being a minor, her real name was never disclosed) both had a mother very much hovering in the wings to 'further their daughter's career'. It was not fifteen-year-old Lita who kept a day-by-day diary of Charlie's 'perversions', it was mother. It was not fifteen-year-old Beverly Aadland who wrote a book about her affair with Errol Flynn, it was mother. And it was not thirteen-year-old 'Sandra' who went to the police to complain about being seduced by Polanski; again, it was mother.

Hollywood Lolita's mother is a vital figure in the Humbert–Lolita relationship because it is usually *her* ambition which is the motive power behind her daughter's precocious use of her sex appeal to get where and what she wants. This can take on semi-innocent forms: the three-year-old Jodie Foster baring her rather provocative white bottom to show off her tan line in a tanning-lotion commercial; or Brooke Shields posing nude at ten in photographs erotic enough for her to try extremely hard a few years later to get them taken off the market. Hollywood Lolita's mother often seeks vicarious success through her daughter, determined the girl will succeed where she has failed, or partially failed. It is no coincidence that Lita McMurray's mother was a very minor actress. So was the mother of Polanski's 'Sandra'. So was Elizabeth Taylor's mother. So was Judy Garland's. So was Brooke Shields'. For all these women it was too late to claw their way to the top, so they wanted to make sure that their daughters started in really good time. This sometimes led to so much shoving and pushing that it ended in hatred on the daughter's part.

Hollywood Lolita is eternally young, yet

as old as the cinema itself. We find her tripping through the earliest Biograph one-reeler, neither child nor woman but a little of both, pre-pubescent, pubescent or post-pubescent, but radiating her nymphet magic: half-way between babyhood and womanhood, girl-child pretending to be vamp through grown-up attitudes and reactions, or else young woman turning herself back into little girl through childish clothing and posturing. We meet her in all her guises, from the most chastely naïve to the most sexually explicit, pouting, simpering, shyly or coyly smiling, across some eight decades of cinema. Despite our disapproval, exasperation or even contempt for her wiles, she lures us on through the years, in black and white or glorious Technicolor, soundlessly or talkie-wise. And we have to admit – even reluctantly – that Hollywood Lolita is often irresistible. She is often in dubious taste, yet as Nabokov insisted, 'vulgarity does not necessarily impair certain mysterious characteristics, the fey grace, the elusive, shifty, soul-shattering, insidious charm'.

LILLIAN GISH
Hollywood's earliest – and chastest – nymphet, whose Dresden-like beauty was either worshipped from afar or slavered over by lecherous Humberts

MABEL NORMAND
The cute dimpled innocent was really a secret junkie who ruined her life with dope-filled peanuts

MARY MILES MINTER
An angel of girlish purity whose little pink silk nightie was discovered in the closet of murdered Desmond Taylor Morris

MARY PICKFORD
'America's sweetheart' played plucky ten-year-olds till well into her thirties though off-screen she was a sophisticated divorcee and businesswoman

2. The Sexual Victorians

Mary Pickford, Lillian and Dorothy Gish, Mae Marsh, Blanche Sweet, Mary Miles Minter and many other child women of the silent screen were the pioneer Hollywood Lolitas. They owe much to their nineteenth-century prototypes, the cloying heroines of the novels of Charles Dickens, since many of the great early film-makers, especially D.W. Griffith and Charlie Chaplin, were fervent admirers of the celebrated novelist and often paid tribute to him in their choice and treatment of subjects on screen. The early film heroine owes everything to the Dickensian heroine, and the fact that Dickens was a young girl-worshipper in real life and in his works doubtless has a lot to do with it.

It was through art that Dickens relived his hopeless longings for unavailable young girls, in his adoring descriptions of Little Nell and a variety of other girl-children or child-women such as Flo Dombey, Little Dorrit, Amy, Dora, Little Emily, and others. Edgar Allan Poe (another nineteenth century writer whom Griffith passionately admired) relived his incestuous and paedophilic love for his thirteen-year-old cousin in *Annabel Lee* (a poem which haunted Griffith and Nabokov's Humbert Humbert). Lewis Carroll's sensuously lovely photographs of girl-children sublimated his obsession for the Alices he could not possess, not even in Wonderland. Over and over again, the puritanical Griffith, through his screen male brutes, came within a hair's breadth of possessing the young actresses he loved – perhaps chastely – in real life. In film after film, Chaplin, as the Little Tramp, worshipped from afar the youngsters that the celebrated actor had no trouble seducing off-screen. Erich Von Stroheim revealed far more about his repressed longings when his hero pressed schoolgirl Kitty's knickers to his lips in *Queen Kelly* than when he depicted more overt screen seductions of maturer women.

Little Nell and her Victorian sisters transmitted to the early Hollywood heroines a petite beauty, a saintly precocity, a threatened innocence, and above all that quality of 'littleness', relating not only to physical size but to something else as well. The adjective was milked to death by the silent film-makers. The *Oxford Dictionary* specifies that 'little' has 'emotional implications not given by "small".' A Dickensian scholar explained that in Dickens, the word 'little' 'is never merely factual, but serving to add an emotional sweetening'. How true this concept of 'emotional sweetening' was to prove later, in the days of *Little* Mary Pickford, *Little* Mary Miles Minter, and *Little* Blanche Sweet! Among Pickford film titles, we encounter: *Little Pal, The Poor Little Rich Girl, The Little Princess, Little Lord Fauntleroy, Such a Little Queen* and *Little Annie Rooney*. But the addiction to sugar was to survive well into the talkies. Sample of the titles of Shirley Temple films: *Our Little Girl,. The Littlest Rebel, The Little Colonel*, and so on.

The word 'child' was fraught with emotional connotations in early twentieth century movies when the child in question happened to be an almost nubile female. For many of the 'children' depicted by the early Hollywood film-makers were not really children at all so much as ambivalent creatures, children in terms of years, adults in terms of character, or else the other way round: adolescents in terms of years but child-like in appearance and character. They were tiny and baby-faced. They had huge eyes and long curly hair. Their expression was winsome, wistful, frightened or pouting, but it always reflected the reactions of children unused to the ways of the world.

Two versions of the silent movie nymphet formula. Left: Lillian Gish, the eternal victim. Below: Edna Purviance, the wistful, sun-kissed country maiden.

Their stage names could reflect this – Louise Lovely, Blanche Sweet, Arline Pretty. Even if their names were ordinary (Mary Pickford, Mabel Normand, Edna Purviance), on the silent film title cards they were referred to as 'The Waif', 'Little Sister', 'The Dear One', 'The Friendless One', 'The Little Disturber', 'The Child', 'Little Miss Yes'm' or 'Little Flora'. Like some Dickens heroines, they might be crippled (Dorothy Gish in *Judith of Bethulia*, Mary Pickford in *Stella Maris*), or else blind (Dorothy Gish again in *Orphans of the Storm*, Virginia Merrill in *City Lights*); physical handicap (or mental, as in *Foolish Wives*) underlined their helplessness and need of masculine protection. But it was enough for a girl to look ridiculously weak, however staunch her spirit, to be diminutive in size (camera angles always stressed the smallness), to be absurdly young (lighting effects were used to make her seem even younger than her years), and clearly not cut out to fend for herself in a world of villainy and harshness. Silent movie heroines had to project in purely visual terms a combination of sexual innocence and desirability, and the easiest way to do this was again to stress her extreme youth – she had to be a nymphet.

At this time there were two distinct yet overlapping types of Hollywood Lolita: the comedy Lolita and the tragedy Lolita. The urchin and the waif. The cute and the pathetic. Both were child-like, but coped with dramatic situations in the different ways called for by their persona: Lillian Gish by grovelling on her knees and pleading for mercy in *Broken Blossoms*, Mae Marsh by hurling herself off a cliff to escape her pursuer in *Birth of a Nation*, or Mary Pickford boldly freeing all the stray dogs from the back of the wicked dog-catcher's wagon in *The Foundling*, or saucy Mabel Normand kicking her over-presumptuous swain into submission in *Mabel's Busy Day*. Both varieties of nymphet had to handle difficult, often perilous situations, usually at the hands of overbearing, sometimes lecherous men much larger and stronger than themselves. But the approach differed according to genre. The childish heroine's

struggle against a hard world was intended to draw tears in some cases, laughter in others.

The tragedy Lolitas tended to be more fragile and Dresden-like than the comedy Lolitas. Lillian Gish was one of many, but she exemplified the type of girl who evolved in 'a world in which beastly men and gallant men vie with each other for the chance to debauch or protect women', as Ethan Mordden put it in his book, *Movie Star*. The comedy Lolita could be more bouncy and plump, as long as it was puppy-fat, like Mabel Normand, the Mack Sennett girl and heroine of countless early Chaplin two-reelers: 'A big-eyed, buxom, bubbling beauty – five feet of fun'. Buxomness and bubbles were acceptable as long as the heroine was a teenager (Mabel was seventeen) and undersized. This was also true of Edna Purviance and Gloria Swanson in her Mack Sennett bathing beauty days. The 'Little Mary' (Miles Minter or Pickford) tragi-comic Lolita type could look a bit less fragile than her tragedy counterpart, but dared have no

such secondary sexual characteristics as
Mabel's ripe bust or Edna's round bottom.
Ideally, she wore rags or pinafores, or even
little-boy clothes, that dissimulated the nascent femininity of the body while enhancing
by contrast the prettiness of the face and the
sweetly petulant coquettishness of the expression.

But just as there were legions of Hollywood Lolitas, so the celluloid capital could
boast its very own Humberts, particularly
David Wark Griffith, Charles Chaplin and
Erich von Stroheim.

'The American movie-going public has
the mind of a twelve-year-old child,' D.W.
Griffith once complained, 'it must have life
as it isn't.' This was in many ways fortunate
for America's first and perhaps greatest film-
maker; for despite his tremendous creative
genius, Griffith too had 'the mind of a
twelve-year-old' as far as his approach to the
movie heroine was concerned. He too
wanted 'life as it isn't' when he portrayed his
delectable girl heroines, and this coincidence of wishful fantasy between film-

maker and movie audiences goes a long way
to explain how someone as artistic, sensitive
and technically *avant-garde* as Griffith
could at the same time be so popular.

David Wark Griffith was born in 1875,
and was thus already twenty-five years old
by the end of the nineteenth century, a true
Victorian in every sense of the word. Born in
Kentucky, he was the son of a Southern
officer, brought up on tales of old Southern
gallantry and *ante-bellum* romance. His
tastes in literature and many of his ideas for
his later films were drawn from nineteenth
century literature, especially those of Dickens, George Eliot, the Brontë sisters and
Bret Harte. His favourite poets were Alfred
Tennyson and Browning, whose tales he
used for four of his films. Above all, he loved
the works of fellow-Southerner, Edgar Allan
Poe, husband and soon widower of a thirteen-year-old girl (though this was less rare
or strange in the South of the United States
than elsewhere; to this day, thirteen is still
the legal age of consent in certain Southern
states). One of Griffith's very first films was a

life of Edgar Allan Poe.

Griffith made his first picture in 1908. It was called *The Adventures of Dolly*, and what is more helpless, less autonomous than a doll? His Dolly was a little girl stolen by gypsies. She was not finally recovered from them until the water cask in which she had been hidden had fallen off a waggon into the river, where it was carried off by a strong downstream current, over a waterfall, through seething rapids. All the Griffith elements were already present in this two-reeler: the hapless, friendless pubescent girl orphan, victim of the elements and of men's cruelty and cupidity.

From the way Griffith treated his girl heroines on screen (and sometimes off for the purpose of shooting certain difficult scenes) one might think that he was a woman-hater, settling his score with womankind through his artistic medium. Lillian Gish was realistically beaten to death by a sadistic boxer in *Broken Blossoms*; she narrowly avoided rape in *Hearts of the World* as well as in *Birth of a Nation*. In the latter film, Mae Marsh was less fortunate and paid with her life to escape a similar fate. Carol Dempster too had a bad time at the hands of an evil German in *The Girl Who Stayed at Home*, then at the hands of an evil Chinaman in *Dream Street*. There were whippings, attempted rape and murder in store for Lillian Gish in *The Greatest Question*, and again in *Orphans of the Storm*, as well as in numberless other lesser-known Griffith two-reelers. That the villains who perpetrated such acts were frequently muscular blacks, Asians, Germans or Frenchmen has often led to the accusation that Griffith was a chauvinist and a racist, though the demands of the story and the visual impact of 'exotic' villains required by the silent movie may partly explain such sexual stereotyping. That the bad guy was so often a villainous-looking middle-aged brute of sanguinary appearance, while the girl's rescuer, if there was one, was usually a clean-cut, fresh-faced, much younger man, was also characteristic of Victorian melodrama. But one cannot avoid wondering if this triangle – bestial older man, pure-minded younger

man, and the half-grown girl over whom they fight – was not the symbolic re-enactment of Griffith's own inner struggle against his sexual urges. The good and gallant Southern gentleman in him fighting it out with the aging lecher. The urge to sully and defile in raging conflict with the urge to worship and adore.

It is not only today that we are startled by the sexual sadism in Griffith's films as well as by his talent and obvious love for his maltreated heroines. As early as 1920, the motion-picture critic of *Photoplay* was already complaining about what he considered 'Griffith's obsession with scenes in which women and girls are beaten or attacked'. Even the director's most fervent admirer, Edward Wagenknecht, had to admit: 'Nobody would deny that Griffith overworked the situation of the innocent heroine menaced by the lascivious monster.'

Yet it is obvious that Griffith did worship and adore his girl heroines, however ill-treated they were in his films. In the true

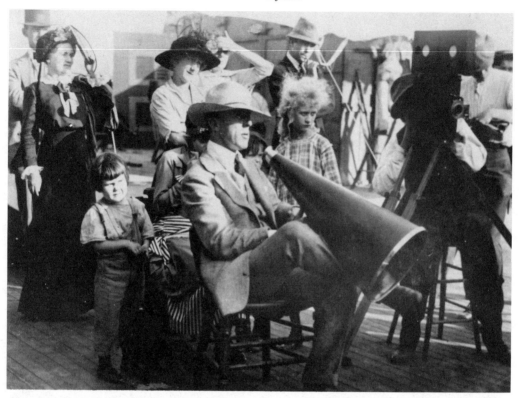

spirit of old-fashioned gallantry, he set them up on a pedestal, he lovingly photographed them in close-up, dwelling on their tremulous smiles, their flowing hair, their huge eyes which glistened with tears or with subdued childish mirth. He called his films after them: *Broken Blossoms*, *The Love Flower*, *The White Rose*. He gave them names like White Almond Flower, the Dear One, Brown Eyes ... In *Broken Blossoms*, Chinky creates a shrine for his 'White Blossom' and quite literally worships the little girl who cradles a doll.

Many people have compared Griffith's relationship with the girls he turned into actresses with that of Svengali and Trilby or Pygmalion and Galatea. Yet the creator's feelings for his creation is always ambivalent. As one feminist writer said of Griffith: 'He created an artistically whole universe where the impulse to degrade his Galateas was inseparable from the impulse to elevate them.' But his Galateas were grateful and they too placed him on a pedestal. 'Anything

he told me to do, I did,' Blanche Sweet later recalled, 'anything to win his praises.' Anything? Mary Pickford, both Gish sisters, Mae Marsh, Bessie Love, Colleen Moore and Carol Dempster would doubtless have agreed. Their submission to the master was legendary. They were delighted to respond to his expectations, to act the little girl for him in his films and in real life, even when they were somewhat over-age. Wagenknecht described going to a first local showing of *Sally of the Sawdust*. Griffith 'called Carol Dempster out from the wings. "Say good evening to the ladies and gentlemen," he told her, as if she had been a little girl appearing at the last-day-of-school exercises in the second grade. Carol responded in character by piping, "Good evening, ladies and gentlemen," and that was about it.' The force of Griffith's artistic personality and genius, his prestige and very real power as Hollywood's most respected film director for twenty years obviously helped. But the fact that he was tall, paternal, soft-spoken

and elegant must have also gone a long way to explain his extraordinary hold over the inexperienced girls he used in his films.

That Griffith's inner sexual and emotional conflicts regarding his girls were vital to his art is also obvious. The dual relationship implied by the powerful older man manipulating much younger women is repeated over and over again in Hollywood's history – with Griffith, Charlie Chaplin, Errol Flynn, Polanski, and any number of other celebrated actors and film-makers. It is that of the surrogate father/surrogate daughter, when a debutante actress comes under the influence of an experienced director or leading man (often her big daddy and first lover as well), and is transposed on-screen in a Lolita/Humbert projection.

Griffith was in his late thirties when he began in earnest to gather round himself at Biograph Studios a posy of dainty girls who, already extremely young, all looked about five years younger than their real age; when they started out with him, Blanche Sweet was seventeen, Mary Pickford nineteen, Lillian and Dorothy Gish sixteen and fourteen respectively, Colleen Moore fifteen, and Mae Marsh seventeen. The real wonder of it all is

that no-one actually knows what his true relationship was with them. Those who have claimed to know for sure were only pretending. There might still be some diminutive old ladies in their eighties left who could elucidate the mystery, but none have so far. A few have dropped hints, particularly about the acknowledged favourite, Lillian Gish, but they were only hints. Griffith called Lillian 'the most beautiful blonde in the world'. But even the cynical Anita Loos declared that no-one 'ever dared whisper that their association was anything but platonic'.

Griffith had to be very cautious indeed to avoid scandal. The actress, Linda Arvidson, had been his wife since 1905, and though they did not get along and separated after 1911, she refused a divorce; it was hinted that she blackmailed her husband for many years, threatening to expose his affairs with some of his leading ladies unless he paid her substantial sums of money. Unlike Humbert Humbert's spouse, she refused to die conveniently to leave the way open for Griffith in his sublimated quest for an ideal Lolita.

Later authors called the great director 'a notorious womanizer', or spoke of his 'obsession, on screen and off, with young female children'. But it all remained pretty vague, and it is almost more intriguing to assume that the courteous Southern gentleman really did respect the youth and virtue of his girls. Imbued with chivalrous notions of gallantry and morality, Griffith was notorious in his day not for his affairs, but for the puritanical atmosphere that prevailed on his sets. He shot some of the most erotic sequences ever to appear on a screen, erotic because they so vividly portrayed suppressed lust and the pangs of unfulfilled desire. Yet he was scandalized when Marguerite Clark peeled off her stockings in *Wildflower*. Flirting was frowned upon on set, let alone bad language, and people did not call each other by their Christian names. So much so that when, in later years, Lillian Gish wrote her autobiography, it was entitled: *The Movies, Mr Griffith And Me*, though she had

worked with the great director for a decade, and had gone out with him on countless private occasions.

Movies seem to have come a long way since Griffith's time. Or have they? Sex is about desire rather than its fulfilment; fulfilment results only in loss of interest, temporarily at least. The more protracted the desire, the more sustained the excitement. And Griffith knew a thing or two about desire and its portrayal. The opening caption of his remake of *The Battle of the Sexes* reads: 'This Battle rages always and shall always for the struggle of desire pursued and desire running away, with or against its will struggling.' A declaration genteelly put, left tantalizingly vague, yet seething with Griffithian lust, both given rein to and kept in check.

It was in *Broken Blossoms* that the enactment of 'desire pursued and desire running away, with or against its will struggling' reached a frenzied crescendo, in scenes that are rightly famous for their quivering sensuality and their torrid atmosphere, despite the fact that nothing happens in them. The silent movies' Hollywood Lolita reached her artistic and erotic summit in this story, originally called 'The Chink and the Child', drawn from Thomas Burke's *Limehouse Nights*. The fact that Lillian Gish impersonates a twelve-year-old, that she plays all the love scenes clutching a large doll (the baby she is supposed to be too young to bear?), that no portion of her body is ever revealed though she spends much of the time lying on a bed, epitomizes Griffith's obsessions: even if one does not share them, their intensity is almost frightening. The story of an adoring Chinaman who takes in a brutalized little girl and moans with longing for her as she lies asleep or innocently plays, sometimes almost (but never quite) giving in to his passion, symbolizes the sexual conduct and standards Griffith either adopted for himself or would have wished to adopt. Several of the scenes are strangely similar to those depicted in the early chapters of *Lolita*, before Humbert Humbert has any hope of possessing his nymphet, as she

alternately sleeps and plays.

In his next film, *The Greatest Question* (1919), Griffith once again dressed up Lillian Gish as a child, gave her a doll to hug, and called her Little Miss Yes'm. But this time she was lusted over by a hideous, middle-aged brute (Humbert Humbert in another guise?); his name was Cain and he lived in 'The House of Darkness'. Too innocent to understand what he really wanted until it was almost too late, Miss Yes'm had to be rescued by a clean-cut, chaste-looking young man. Chinky, who almost swooned with suppressed desire, Mr Cain, who slavered with obscene, unhidden lust, and the upright young fellow who came to Little Miss Yes'm's rescue, were all facets of Griffith's own complex temperament. We shall never know which of the three prevailed in his dealings with his girls. But we do know that, at sixty-one, when he was at last free to do so, he married a twenty-six-year-old actress he had known since she was thirteen. As for Lillian Gish, 'the most beautiful blonde in the world', who could have

had any man for the asking, she never married and remained officially as virginal as on the day she met 'the Shakespeare of the Screen'. Another motion picture pioneer, Mack Sennett, said: 'D.W. Griffith invented the movies.' It can also be said that Griffith invented Hollywood Lolita.

'We don't know enough to get married,' Little Miss Yes'm coyly replied to the young suitor who proposed to her after rescuing her in *The Greatest Question*. Coming from a nubile young miss who has just barely escaped rape, this remark sounds a little preposterous even though Lillian Gish was meant to be about thirteen years old. Are we really to believe that young girls were so ignorant back in those days? According to Colleen Moore, who was briefly a Griffith girl at fifteen before turning into the screen's first 'flapper', they were. 'Most fifteen-year-olds today, I suppose, know the so-called facts of life. I and my girlfriends at the studio didn't know them and wouldn't have dreamed of asking anyone. Sex, if it was spoken of at all, was something whispered ... we were fully as innocent as the heroines we portrayed.' Yet at another point in her autobiography, Miss Moore admits perhaps more frankly: 'The Victorian influence still persisted. Girls were innocent and unsophisticated, or if they weren't they pretended to be, because this was the accepted, the ideal image.'

Innocence and unsophistication were thus an ideal, an expectation, an image to be projected on a screen rather than necessarily a reality for all. In private, from inclination or to further their careers, very young girls were not above using their sex appeal, sometimes actually harassing influential men who could get them into the movies. At twelve, Bebe Daniels had managed to charm several Sennett Studio directors into giving her Bathing Beauty parts. When Sennett himself ('The Old Man', as he was always called) decreed that she was too young and fired her, she used her charms on Harold Lloyd and obtained a leading role from him when she was only thirteen. Mabel Nor-

mand was an artist's model at thirteen. Mack Sennett has described his alarm when, one day, he interviewed a young thing for a part: 'I said "Let's see your knees, honey" like a banker might ask a client for a look at the collateral – you know, strictly business. She heisted her dress all the way up and spun around buff-naked.' Sennett's dismay on this occasion can be believed, for he never claimed to have been a saint in other circumstances. His casting couch was notorious, and he himself admitted when speaking of would-be Bathing Beauties: 'They were dollipers, all of them, and the man who wouldn't reach for one of them, or a handful of them – well, there is no possible way to describe a man who never existed.'

None of which quite tallies with Colleen Moore's declaration that she and her girlfriends at the studio 'didn't know the facts of life', nor her supposed naïveté at fifteen, which the following anecdote illustrates: 'One day, I overheard an older actress talking to a friend who'd been given a star part by a well-known director. "Of course,"

she said maliciously, "she paid the price." I wondered how big the price was and if my father could afford to buy a part like that for me.' What the story *does* prove is that even if young Colleen Moore couldn't understand what the price was, other girls were prepared to pay it. What mattered was to appear innocent and virtuous on-screen. But audiences were still Victorian enough also to expect a girl to live up to this pretence in her private life, and Heaven help her if she got found out. Two of Hollywood's freshest blossoms, Mabel Normand and Mary Miles Minter would soon discover how puritanical America still was, and how pure it expected its girl stars to be.

At the time, Mabel Normand was Hollywood's most popular comedienne, a Mack Sennett girl (and the mistress of 'the Old Man' since her mid-teens), and Charlie Chaplin's first leading lady in such celebrated classics as *Mabel's Strange Predicament*, *Mabel at the Wheel*, *Mabel's Busy Day*, *Mabel's Married Life*, *His Trysting Place*, *Tillie's Punctured Romance*, *Getting Acquainted*, and other early Chaplin comedies. Minter was one of the most angelical-

ly pretty and virginal-looking nymphets ever to grace a screen. A child star at four in the theatre, she had been a film star since the age of twelve. In one of her films (*The Fairy and the Waif*, 1914) she was described by one critic as 'exquisitely fascinating, sympathetically charming, and delightfully childlike'. Like her rival, Mary Pickford, she was tiny, blue-eyed and golden-haired, and obviously cut out to go on playing child-parts well into her thirties. But fate intervened.

At seventeen, she confided in her pal Colleen Moore that she was tired of being treated like a child of six. She longed for a little bit of experience and true-life romance. This was no easy ambition, with her Studio out to protect its virginal asset and her mother constantly on her heels. Mary's mother, Charlotte Shelby, never let her daughter out of her sight if she could help it. 'This eagle-eyed surveillance didn't exactly stem from mother love ... the thought of losing this gold-mine daughter to a husband filled Mama with such terror she became almost insanely jealous,' was Colleen Moore's impression. This is the typical Hollywood Lolita's mother, repeated countless times over Hollywood's history and still going strong.

Colleen and Mary sometimes managed to slip off together on innocent double dates with boys their own age when Mama wasn't looking. But most of the time she was looking. However, she was less disapproving when her daughter started visiting the prominent film director, William Desmond Taylor. Surely, at forty-five he was much too old and gentlemanly to try and seduce a mere child, and besides Charlotte was having an affair with him herself, as it emerged at the trial that was to follow. When Mary wrote to Taylor, she always called him her 'Dearest Daddy' and signed 'Blessed Baby'. Taylor's butler, Henry Peavy, later described how Mary would ask him: 'How is Mr Taylor, Henry? The reason I ask you is because Mr Taylor is just like a father to me.' When the young actress gave Taylor a photograph of herself, it was coldly and respectfully inscribed: 'For William Desmond

Faithfully Yours
Mary Miles Minter

Witzel
Art

Taylor, artist, gentleman, Man! Sincere good wishes, Mary Miles Minter, 1920.'

Whatever the real nature of their relationship, no-one would ever have been any the wiser if Taylor had not been brutally murdered on February 1st, 1922. The mystery killer who shot him in the back was never found. He – or was it she? – calmly slipped out of the house as soon as the deed was done and vanished into the night. The murder of so widely-respected a figure as Taylor sent shock waves through Hollywood, and the resulting inquiry caused a furore greater than the murder itself. It revealed a tale of false identity, theft, bootlegging, drugs and strange sexual involvements. It also revealed that Taylor had been a Humbert Humbert figure to Mary Miles Minter, who had felt a consuming passion for her 'dearest daddy'. Her love letters to him were found in the toe of his boots; a little pink silk nightgown, with the intials MMM embroidered in the centre of the yoke, hung in the closet of his bedroom. What made it even more shocking was that Mary did nothing to deny or cover up the evidence. She arrived on the scene as soon as the murder was discovered, clawed her way through the police lines, sobbing and proclaiming her undying love for the victim. She told the police that yes, she and Taylor had been in love and were planning to marry the moment she was of age and could get away from her mother's clutches. She declared touchingly but unwisely: 'It was simply a beautiful white flame. I had always been a reserved, very retiring girl, and he was the first man and the only man who ever embodied all the glories of manhood in one private body. He represented that to me.'

All this was quite steamy enough to keep the story on the front page of every newspaper day after day. But instead of dying down, the story grew more and more bizarre and sensational as time passed. First of all, could Mary's mother have been the murderer? The only person to have caught a glimpse of the killer was to declare at the preliminary hearing: 'There was something about the man's appearance that didn't sit right. A cap was pulled well down over his

face, a muffler hiding the lower half. The suit on his short body looked bunchy.' Under oath, the witness, a neighbour, testified that the man looked more like a woman dressed as a man.

Or might the murderer have been Mabel Normand, another of Taylor's many young lady-friends? She was the last person to have seen him alive, only half an hour before he was shot. It was unlikely, but speculation, intimation and insinuation ran rife. What did emerge and help to wreck Mabel's career was that she was a drug addict and was being blackmailed by the drug ring that kept her supplied in cocaine-filled peanuts. Taylor had supposedly tried to break up the ring and to help Mabel kick the habit; or was he buying the peanuts for her? She was carrying a big bag of them on the night of the murder.

Mabel was cleared of any direct involvement in the murder and her connection with the drug ring was never proven. Yet that didn't stop women's clubs all across America from passing resolutions to boycott her films for good. Virtuous citizens were

hood sweetheart had haunted Nabokov's Humbert. The poverty-stricken boy emigrated to America, became one of the world's wealthier citizens entirely through his genius and his business acumen, but the girls he loved never got any older, culminating in his marriage to seventeen-year-old Oona O'Neil, Eugene O'Neil's daughter, when Chaplin himself was fifty-four.

Charlie Chaplin was rich and famous within a short time after he began his Hollywood film career. Dressed in a well-cut suit and without the joke moustache, he was also very handsome. This would have been quite enough to draw hordes of girls to him, even the very young ones he liked best. But he exerted a further attraction, which made him completely irresistible. As Parker Tyler put it in his *Chaplin: Last of the Clowns*, 'His very practise of making "finds" among the would-be actresses that thronged the gates of Hollywood studios was an advertisement to girls who had heard of his extreme susceptibility to feminine charm.'

Back in 1918, Chaplin only just averted disaster in his relationship with Mildred Harris, a wide-eyed innocent with long blonde curls in the true silent-movie tradition of fragile girl-children. Mildred was only fourteen when the 'little tramp' met her, and had just turned sixteen when he got her pregnant; Chaplin had to whisk her across the Mexican border in all haste to make an honest woman of her, thus avoiding scandal and prosecution by a hair's breadth. All it cost him in the end was a hefty settlement when he got divorced from his child bride a year and a half later, and a humiliating punch-up with Louis B. Mayer, who had Mildred under contract. Humiliating, because Mayer publicly called him a 'filthy pervert' and then knocked him down in the middle of a fashionable restaurant.

There were doubtless many other unknown nymphets in Chaplin's life over the next few years, but the one who was to cause him big, big trouble was a certain Lilita McMurray. Was she the model for the original Lolita, as some have suggested? Chaplin had first met her when she was seven years old at Kitty's Come-On Inn

not to go and laugh at the antics of a drug addict, or to delight in the on-screen virginity of a girl who left her nightie in a dirty old man's closet. Mary Miles Minter soon had to sue her mother for the million dollars she had earned in her heyday and which seemed to have been stashed away so carefully by Mama that they had disappeared without trace. Mabel became more ill than ever of the tuberculosis that was to kill her a few years later. Taylor's death had put an end to three careers, not one. The American public had made it clear that it expected its favourite stars to behave themselves, or at least not to get found out.

America had scarcely had the time to recover from the William Desmond Taylor murder trial when another nymphet scandal broke out, involving the most famous film star of all time: Charlie Chaplin. The 'little fellow' was always obsessed with very young girls. His unrequited passion for a fifteen-year-old actress called Hetty Kelly when he himself was still a teenager haunted him throughout his adult existence, as a child-

(Nabokov would have loved that name too). She was the daughter of one of the waitresses, Nana, a frustrated actress (what else?). Enthusiastically encouraged by Nana, Lilita soon became 'great friends' with the already world-famous comedian. Her reward was work as a child extra in Chaplin's films; Nana's reward was that she could give up waiting on tables to supervise her daughter's career.

At twelve, Lilita played an angel in *The Kid*, and it was around this time that Nana

Charlie Chaplin was one of the most adored men in Hollywood. Nubile starlets flocked to be discovered by him, some at their peril. However, his penchant for

young girls did not interfere with his cinematic ambitions – in fact he combined the two most successfully, as his leading ladies would testify.

started complaining that the Little Tramp was trying to turn her baby into a little tramp. Tongues began wagging busily in Hollywood, and Chaplin would have done well to vanish from Lilita's life forever; but somehow he couldn't bring himself to give her up. Nobody knows at what age and under what conditions their affair began: who seduced who, or what part Nana really played. The fact is that when Lilita had just turned fifteen, she too had to be rushed across the Mexican border and hastily married because she was pregnant.

Again, a nymphet had been turned into an honest woman in the nick of time. Hounded by reporters, tut-tutted by fans and friends, Charlie is said to have muttered on the wedding-night train trip back to Los Angeles: 'Well, boys, this is better than the penitentiary, but it won't last.'

He was right. Nana instantly moved in with her daughter and new son-in-law and busily started meddling in their life, turning the house into a permanent open party for her friends and relatives, and above all spying upon Charlie's every word and deed.

Two years and two babies later, Lita filed for divorce; Chaplin – and the world – discovered what had really been going on under his roof: Nana, briefed by her obedient daughter, had kept a day-by-day account recording every intimate detail of the marriage that could be damaging to Chaplin. Every grievance, every unorthodox sexual demand, every salacious remark now appeared in court and in print, even the charge that Chaplin had forced his child-wife to listen to him read aloud passages from the monstrous *Lady Chatterly's Lover*!

That the whole ghastly mess did not wreck Chaplin's career, though he was crucified by many a newspaper columnist, proves that the nineteenth century double standard still prevailed in twentieth century Hollywood: Mary Miles Minter and Mabel Normand were guilty of far less 'moral turpitude', but they were girls, so they were automatically tainted. Apart from a full-scale nervous breakdown and a million dollars or so to settle on his Lilita and her calculating mother, Chaplin escaped relatively unscathed. He only suffered a temporary loss of popularity, but when he finally got back to work a few months later on *The Circus* his hair had grown so white that it had to be dyed black to play the Little Fellow.

Mary Pickford was one Hollywood Lolita who led a charmed existence. Though William Desmond Taylor had directed some of her films and was a close friend, his strange murder did not smear 'America's Sweetheart'. Not even divorce and remarriage would come between Mary Pickford and her fans. She was said to have 'The most beloved face in the world'. Words today cannot begin to convey the impact of Mary Pickford on film audiences of her time. She was the world's sweetheart, not only America's. Colleen Moore, a few years younger than the great Mary, describes asking her mother at the outbreak of World War I if Mary couldn't put an end to hostilities just by going over to Europe to reason with the Kaiser. As Wagenknecht wrote to her in a open letter of wonderment and adoration: 'Your own personality cast a

Right: *Two of the screen's greatest names, Mary Pickford and Charlie Chaplin, combined business with pleasure, cashing in on their popularity to found United Artists.*

madonna-like exaltation about you, and the roles you often played made you our mischievous child.'

But Mary had rivals: some found Mary Miles Minter more doll-like and virginal; others thought Marguerite Clark daintier (like Pickford, she was under five feet tall and playing child roles until well into her thirties, among them *The Prince and the Pauper* in boys' clothing and little Eva in *Uncle Tom's Cabin*). May McAvoy's admirers pointed to their favourite's more wistful and spiritual qualities, and there were those who whispered that the Gish sisters were better actresses. But Mary Pickford was unique all the same, occupying a special position in the hearts of all those Americans who shrank from the looming Jazz Age and its baggage of new attitudes and emancipated flappers. Mary has often been called Hollywood's first star: the star system began when the public started demanding 'the girl with the curl' in 1909. Before then, screen actors and actresses had been all but nameless and anonymous. It had not yet occurred to anyone that a film could be constructed round a given individual and be sold on the basis of one person's face and personality. For over two decades, Mary Pickford was Hollywood's greatest star, as well as its first, more popular even than Charlie Chaplin and Douglas Fairbanks, the two megastars with whom she founded United Artists.

Who was Mary Pickford? The question would once have seemed superfluous, even preposterous. *Everyone* knew who she was, that she had originally been called Gladys Smith and that she came from Canada. Everyone knew her latest film and her next film, and what she liked for tea. But poor Little Mary was like poor Little Nell: completely forgotten in later years, or else ridiculed when remembered. She had everything going for her: youth, beauty, charm and the adoring adulation of her contemporaries. Both her strength and her weakness resided in the fact that she belonged utterly to her time. The price to be paid for that particular gift was to be left behind when the times changed, so that when she turned in the course of time into a

bed-ridden recluse, sipping gin, there was nobody left to know or to care.

Mary Pickford was born in 1893 and started her career so young she can scarcely be said to have had a childhood at all. Well before her teens, she was supporting a fatherless brother and sister, as well as the ubiquitous Hollywood mother. As her later producer, Adolph Zucker, once groaned: 'Mary, sweetheart, I don't have to diet. Every time I talk over a new contract with you and your mother I lose ten pounds.' Luckily, Mary had a keen eye for business from the start and was not deprived of her youthful earnings by an over-loving parent as were so many of Hollywood's baby stars. As Mack Sennett put it starkly but tactfully: 'Mary was gracious ... but she was all business. Even then as a dimpled darling, all peaches and cream and very young, Miss Pickford had a bright eye for a dollar.'

Little Mary started off as a Griffith girl in 1909 and stayed with 'God' (as some called him) until 1913. She later claimed to have left Griffith because he 'always wanted to have me running round trees and pointing

*you're not a little girl any more, a good
way to go on looking like one is to
continue cuddling up to them. They won't
know the difference.*

at rabbits'. A girl of principles, she once declared to him: 'I will not exaggerate, Mr Griffith. I think it's an insult to the audience.' Not that this ever prevented her from running round trees and pointing at rabbits in her post-Griffith films. The truth was that Mary didn't want to be anybody's girl – not even Griffith's – off the screen, though she rapidly became everybody's girl in her screen persona. Mary was very much her own girl. She was soon directing her own films, or at least directing her directors, writing her own scripts, selecting her stories and roles as she saw fit, until, logically, she became her own producer the day she created her own studio, United Artists, in 1920. She wanted total artistic control and she got it. Even when she had celebrated directors like Ernest Lubitsch on her payroll, she used them mainly for crowd scenes, tartly reminding Lubitsch when he got uppity that he was working *for* her rather than *with* her. This hard-nosed professionalism was a long way from the brainless innocence of the typical nymphet, yet on-screen, Little Mary played dimpled darling Hollywood Lolita to the hilt, or at least a cute, coy, curly, cherubic version of her, in tune with her times, but still fitting snugly into Nabokov's description of his nymphet as 'a gaspingly adorable pubescent pet'.

Mary's career spanned over two decades and included at least fifty full-length features. The most famous of them are still

aged or elderly couples who now flock to Disneyland to recapture the golden childhood many of them never had, would then have flocked to Mary's films instead. Not surprisingly, the young Walt Disney dreamed of using Little Mary in a film version of *Alice in Wonderland*, where she would have played Alice in live action against animations of the fairyland characters.

Nevertheless, Mary tired of the situation in the long run. In real life, she loved beautiful, sophisticated clothes, and might have enjoyed showing them off on-screen rather than the eternal rags, pinafores or little-boy overalls. 'I can't stand that sticky stuff, you know. I got so tired of being Pollyanna', Mary confessed many years after it was all over. But the problem was that her fans still wanted Pollyanna and nothing else. When asked in a 1925 *Photoplay* contest what roles they would most like to see Mary play, the response was predictable – *Heidi, Cinderella, Alice in Wonderland* or *Little Red Riding Hood*. Mary was still their fairy-tale child, even though they knew she was already thirty-two. And such was the power of her screen image that her fans even forgave her for getting divorced from her first husband, Owen Moore, to remarry swashbuckling Douglas Fairbanks in 1920. Mary and her Studio quailed in terror at the time, convinced that the public would never stand for it, but it did. Mary and Doug made such an irresistible, all-American couple, such an icon of success, looks and money, that the public was ready for once to overlook the issue of morality. Her fans were far less lenient, however, when Mary bobbed her hair in 1929. 'You would have thought I had murdered someone,' she said later, 'and in a sense I had.' Soon after shearing off her locks, Samson-like, she realized that her power was gone. It was time to call it a day. As she later reminisced in a philosophical mood: 'I left the screen because I didn't want what happened to Chaplin to happen to me. When he discarded the Little Tramp, the Little Tramp turned around and killed him. The little girl made me. I'd already been pigeonholed.'

remembered today, at least by name: *Rebecca of Sunnybrook Farm, Little Annie Rooney, Pollyanna, Daddy Long-Legs, A Poor Little Rich Girl*, and so on. When superstars have an enduring love affair with vast audiences, it is because their desires coincide: Mary loved playing children's roles not only because they made her rich and famous but because they made up for something she had never had: a childhood. As she put it: 'I was forced to live far beyond my years when just a child, now I have reversed the order and I intend to remain young indefinitely.' Her fans loved her in such roles for similar reasons. The middle-

SHIRLEY TEMPLE
The youngest person ever to appear in
'Who's Who', 'Miss Curly Top' outshone,
out-earned and out-dazzled
every adult film star who
risked competing with
her winsome ways

3. The Lollipop Brigade

The most celebrated Hollywood Lolitas of the thirties and forties can be roughly divided into three categories: those whose super-stardoms were over by the time they entered their second decade; those who were box-office stars in their teens; and those whose screen career survived the growing up process, who blossomed from unripe movie nymphets to full-blown Hollywood nymphs at the wave of a mascara wand. Peggy Ann Garner, Jane Withers, Margaret O'Brien and, above all, Shirley Temple, belong to the first category. Deanna Durbin and Gloria Jean are the most famous examples of the second, and Judy Garland and Elizabeth Taylor epitomize the third. It might seem that those who fall into this last category were the luckiest – child stardom to them was merely the ante-chamber to adult super-stardom. But it could also be the prelude to adult super-misery: drugs, booze, nervous breakdowns, chaotic love-lives, chronic health problems, all seemed to be built-in features of the existence of the baby-star-turned-big-star.

Why did this have to be? The former Baby Peggy summed it up so well from bitter experience (and *her* career began at twenty-two months!) that there is probably nothing to add to her assessment of why child stardom usually left horrific scars: 'While adult performers could voluntarily place themselves on the movie capital's slave block, Hollywood's children were given no such option. Too young to vend the product which they soon discovered was themselves, they constituted a commodity in which only grown ups dealt... Spoiled darlings in the eyes of an envious public, we were actually child laborers working to support our families... In the end it became clear no matter how much we loved our parents or wanted to believe that they loved us, our real value to them seemed measured only in terms of performance and earning power... While over the years psychologists and sociologists had written volumes about the dangerous influence movies exerted on the youngsters who frequented them, not one word had been written about the crippling effects that an entire childhood spent working in films could have upon a person.'

To varying degrees, this was true for all the child stars of this period, though some turned out to be much more resilient than others – Shirley Temple managed to have an extremely successful adult career in a completely different field – politics. Yet what could be more demoralizing than to be, or at least to feel, 'all washed up' by the age of twenty – or even ten? What could be harder than becoming 'young adults, trying to put together a mature image from the jagged pieces of a shattered child star', to quote Baby Peggy again? The peculiar thing, however, is that it turned out to be almost harder for those child stars who made it over the hurdle of adolescence and who became grown-up stars to adjust and to survive the stress of the process. Gloria Jean turned waitress, Jane Withers making unglamorous TV commercials for a sink cleaner, Deanna Durbin, a housewife in a remote French village, must sometimes have felt pretty wistful as they flipped the pages of *Modern Screen* and *Photoplay* to gaze at the photos of their contemporaries, Liz, Natalie and Judy, basking in the glory and glitter of showbiz. Yet as the years passed they must also have thought: 'There, but for the grace of God, go I...'

Hollywood Lolita has been around since Hollywood became Hollywood, but the child star was a phenomenon of the 1930s, which began in the twenties and carried on for a while into the forties. Not all the girl

ture as long as possible.

The end-product was a hybrid: a womanish child wise beyond her years yet looking younger than her age, whose ambivalent appeal many would find distasteful today. Deanna Durbin's 'pubescence' has been described by a later critic as 'disturbing, even grating', with Deanna forever playing 'a teen-aged old lady marshalling a band of impotent old men'. A casting director at Universal would say of the ten-year-old Liz Taylor: 'Her eyes are too old. She doesn't have the face of a kid.' In the same fashion, Graham Greene dared to describe the eight-year-old Shirley Temple as 'oddly precocious and voluptuous'. Baby Peggy, herself a hot-house product, immediately detected an ambiguity in the appearance of eleven-year-old Judy Garland: 'She looked too old for a child, but she did not yet have the body of a woman.'

Compared to the explicit films of today, the thirties were still the 'age of innocence' for the little girls involved and for their adoring audiences. The average man enjoying a 'sugar and spice and everything nice' movie starring Shirley Temple, Judy Garland or Elizabeth Taylor, would have been outraged if he had been told the delightful child stirred vague Humbert Humbert longings in him. The average woman would never have admitted that, deep down, the reason she saw so many Gloria Jean or Deanna Durbin movies was in order to revert to a 'my heart belongs to daddy', little-girl status, and to imagine herself a spoilt, petted, adored Lolita leading everybody by the heart-strings. Men and women could together forget the complex problems posed by adult relationships and sexual drives at a nymphet movie of the time, while retaining the sentimental enjoyment that love is supposed to procure. Hollywood's baby stars – the girls in particular – had to pander to this adult longing for 'somewhere over the rainbow', and their performances, their persona, their very manner of singing, dancing or smiling, had to appeal to adult tastes. Inevitably this led to the slightly ambiguous quality of many films made for the popcorn eaters by the lollipop brigade.

stars could be termed nymphets however – they were cute, they were sad, they were certainly exploited, but mostly they were allowed simply to be children. The thirties was the golden age of the kiddy-star picture made for *adults* rather than children. Shirley Temple wasn't usually flirting with little boys her own age but with grown-up men. She wasn't acting up for the lollipop brigade but for their parents. Deanna Durbin later declared that her true fans were not children but adults who wanted to fantasize about their vanished childhood. The 'cinemoppets' of the thirties weren't adults pretending to be children, as they had been in the early Hollywood silents; they were children mimicking adult attitudes, including sex. The hot-house atmosphere of the studios aged them prematurely, while the expectations of the public kept them imma-

In 1926, Mary Pickford played one of her last little-girl roles in *Sparrows*, a brilliant and moving parable of good versus evil, the forces of darkness versus the healing powers of faith and endurance. Beautifully shot in grainy black and white, throughout most of the second half of the movie, dauntless Mary Pickford carried on her back, across alligator-infested swamps and deadly quicksands, a chubby, dimpled, curly-haired moppet of about two who was a dead ringer for Shirley Temple. It wasn't the real thing of course, because Shirley wasn't born until April 23rd, 1928, but it was an interesting prefiguration, bridging the gap between 'the girl with the curl' and 'Miss Curly Top'.

Gertrude Temple took her unborn daughter's career exceedingly seriously. She told us so herself: 'Long before she was born I tried to influence her future life by association with music, art and beauty,' she was to declare. 'Perhaps this prenatal preparation helped make Shirley what she is.' It was never too early to start nurturing the future child-star. Jane Withers' mother, Lavinia, started planning her daughter's career years before the infant was even conceived: mother-to-be Withers made it the sole condition of her marriage to father-to-be Withers that, should they have a daughter, he would not prevent the baby-to-be from becoming a child star. Two previous fiancés had refused Lavinia's condition, but Mr Withers accepted it and the rest, as they say, is history.

It may well be that Mrs Temple saw the prototype 'Miss Curly Top' in *Sparrows*, it may have been the inspiration for her daughter's future hairdo, the famous fifty-six curls described by a later writer as 're-fashioned out of Pickford's cuttings'. Mary Pickford cut off her locks in 1929, just as baby Shirley was busy growing hers; Mary left the movies for good in 1932, the year Shirley entered them. A nice succession of coincidences for the two greatest all-time contenders to the title of 'The World's Best Loved Face' and 'The Ultimate Hollywood Lolita'. That Pickford and Temple were contending for the same throne is made even more apparent by the fact that Temple starred in the remakes of a number of Pickford classics, including *Rebecca of Sunnybrook Farm*, *The Little Princess* and *Poor Little Rich Girl*. Most of Temple's films could have been Pickford vehicles had they been made fifteen years earlier, and vice versa.

Little Mary had always been known as 'America's Sweetheart'. No-one could usurp that title, but when Shirley's career really got going there were attempts to get the new 'girl with the curl' known as 'America's *Little* Sweetheart'. The title did not catch on; it smacked of heiress apparent trying to snatch the crown too soon. Yet each was unique in her own way; Shirley Temple seemed every bit as much of a miracle to her fans as Mary Pickford had to hers. Pickford die-hards could rightly claim that their nymphet sweetheart was more beautiful, more spiritually inspiring and a much better actress. Unconditional Temple worshippers could maintain, however, that their idol was much more than a child star: she was an infant prodigy, so precocious that her youthful talent made her a sort of Mozart of the movie-moppet brigade.

Left and right: *Shirley Temple's 'grown-up'
roles in the* Baby Burlesk *one-reelers were
great favourites with her fans. She was all*

The enormous disparity between the ages at which the Pickford and Temple stardoms all but ended – thirty-two and twelve respectively – is probably more significant than the controversy over their different merits. The conventions of the cinema had changed a lot since the early Hollywood years, when one-time child stars of the stage and the music hall like Marie Prevost, Dorothy Gish and Mary Pickford herself, impersonated celebrated children on the screen: Little Lord Fauntleroy, Little Eva, Pollyanna, Peter Pan, the Prince and the Pauper. According to the nineteenth century tradition to which they belonged, such roles were too important to be left to real children. Though real-life kiddies abounded on the screen, it was in background roles only.

It was Charlie Chaplin who first grasped the true potential of a real child on screen when he starred four-year-old Jackie Coogan in *The Kid* in 1920. Chaplin, himself a former child performer in the theatre, realized how much easier it was to get a convincing performance out of a youngster on a movie set than on a stage. The camera could move round the child; adult actors could adapt their performance to his or her limitations. The director could always cut when things went wrong, make signals to the child during shooting, scold it to make it cry, dangle things off-camera or make strange noises to get an expression of surprise or fear. Even the youngest children could be manipulated to get a wholly convincing performance out of them. Wistful Jackie Coogan proved it, became the overnight darling of movie audiences, and the day of the young adult pretending to be a child was almost over.

Mothers all over America began dreaming of pushing their tot to be the next Shirley Temple and 'Your child should be in the movies' became the standard compliment to pay proud moms. Hedda Hopper, the future gossip columnist, shrewdly described the thousands of would-be mothers of child stars converging on Hollywood in the twenties and thirties 'like a flock of hungry locusts'. 'One look into the eyes of

*of three years old. Her uncompromisingly
named 'More Legs Sweet Trick' take-off of
Marlene Dietrich delighted her audience.*

those women told you what was on their
minds: "If I can get this kid of mine on the
screen, we might just hit it big"... Most of
the women showed no mercy. They took
little creatures scarcely old enough to stand
or speak, and like buck sergeants, drilled
them to shuffle through a dance step or
mumble a song. They robbed them of every
phase of childhood to keep the waves in the
hair, the pleats in the dress, the pink polish
on the nails.'

Very few of those thousands of children
ever made it to the screen. Some eked out a
precarious living for their parents as extras,
'atmosphere' children. A few did very well.
But towering over them all was the most
successful screen 'baby' of all – Shirley
Temple. Her career was nearly over when
she was twelve, and in terms of precocity,
she stands in a league of her own. It is
unlikely that anyone will ever beat some of
the age records she set: the youngest person
ever to appear on a *Time* magazine cover, to
be listed in *Who's Who*, and to get an
Academy Award. Her entire career, though it

glittered for less than a decade, is a Guin-
ness Book of Records dream: she was world
box-office queen for four successive years.
On her official eighth birthday (in fact her
ninth as the studio sliced a year off her age
when she was five), she received more than
135,000 birthday presents, including a baby
kangaroo from Australia. At five, she was
only out-earning her own father; by her
tenth birthday her income was the seventh
highest in America ($9,000 a week, plus
$300,000 per film, plus royalties on all
Shirley Temple products). She starred in
eight full-length movies in 1934 (aged only
six, poor child), and automatically sold half
a million records of her most popular film
songs such as *The Good Ship Lollipop* or
Polly Wolly Doodle, out-selling the top
crooners of the day, Bing Crosby and Nelson
Eddy. During those years, she was the most
photographed human being in the world,
well ahead of President Franklin Roosevelt.
She was getting over 500 fan letters a day at
her peak, and still gets quite a few even
today.

What do these astonishing statistics have
to do with the nymphet syndrome in the
movies? Plenty. Shirley Temple was at one
end of the Lolita age-spectrum, Mary Pickford at the other, yet both were colours of
the same long rainbow. One was too young
and the other too old to provoke sexual
anxiety and soul-searching in their besotted
fans, as they would have if they had been
twelve or thirteen. But at six and twenty-six
respectively, they could play wholesome,
asexual nymphets who appealed to cinema
audiences ever eager to pursue the impossible ideal of eternal youth and innocence.
They seemed to embody an evanescent
quality, young, fresh and dewy. They appeared to have everything youth is supposed to have: pluck, optimism, cheerful-
ness, eagerness to help others, and re-
sourcefulness in the face of adversity. These
were precious dreams to cling to, especially
during the Depression. Adults had got themselves into a sorry mess. Could a little child
lead them out of it? Shirley's films allowed
people to believe in that possibility of
salvation, or at least to forget their own
troubles for an hour or two. In her book
Hollywood Children, former child-star Baby
Peggy wrote: 'The new child that Shirley
symbolized not only underscored the de-
ceptive strength of virtue, but she actually
got things done when adults seemed incap-
able of effecting change. Shirley was anything but passive. Pouting, scolding, singing,
dancing her way through every film, *she* did
the cheering up, *she* was the savior.'

Shirley the Saviour had taken over from
Little Mary the Saviour. But Shirley really
was a young child, and this gave her added
authenticity. After all, Little Mary in real life
was a divorcée who liked money, glamorous
clothes and shiny limousines. Shirley was a
little girl who loved dolls, pets and her
mommy and daddy. 'Darling, when Santa
Claus bundled you up, a joyous doll-baby
package, and dropped you down creation's
chimney, he gave to mankind the dearest
and sweetest Christmas present that ever
gladdened the hearts and stirred the souls of
this weary old world,' gushed Irvin S. Cobb
in terms that might have made baby Jesus

*A man needs a lot of affection and
attention, but a little firmness from Shirley
occasionally does no harm.*

himself jealous; after all it was *His* birthday, not Shirley's. 'God, he made her just all by herself. No series. Just one,' rhapsodized Bill Robinson, the black dancer who was teamed up with her in several films. If only childhood lasted forever, they could have started a thriving Shirley Temple religion.

This idolatry of the star-child was reflected in the box-office and in the profits to be made out of anything connected with the Temple name and face. She earned an estimated $20 million for her studio between 1935 and 1939, and one can scarcely guess how much for all the products marketed in her name: Shirley Temple dolls, dresses, bathing-suits, soaps, ribbons, books, combs, soft toys . . . the list is endless.

When today's TV audiences see a Shirley Temple film on the late late show, they may wonder what all the fuss was about. So how can her appeal be defined? Shirley Temple was undoubtedly a charming little girl, not outrageously beautiful like Elizabeth Taylor or Brooke Shields, but cute in an all-American way; like Debbie Reynolds, Shirley Maclaine or – why not? – Doris Day. She certainly was precocious; one can scarcely disagree with Adolph Menjou, who co-starred with her in *Little Miss Marker*, when he said, 'She knows all the tricks. . . She's an Ethel Barrymore at four.' And it has to be admitted that there is something truly astonishing about a six-year-old who can act, sing and dance so delightfully and consistently through scores of movies.

More than genius or even talent, Shirley's willingness to please and her innate good nature were probably what made her outshine all her rivals. She had been conditioned from her earliest years to give satisfaction and to obey. 'When I speak, she minds. There is no argument, no pleading and begging,' her mother once grimly explained. 'I have never permitted any impudence, crying or display of temper. . . I began this training very early and it means constant vigilance. I soon learned not to let my affection make me too lenient.'

This iron discipline did not turn Shirley into 'The Littlest Rebel', but into a 'Poor Little Rich Girl', a very rich one indeed. Obsessively eager to please her mother, her

first question upon waking up would be: 'What are we going to pretend today?' 'I was determined she should excel at something,' Mrs Temple explained, and what Shirley learned to excel at most was pleasing mother. Allan Dwan, who directed the child in *Heidi* and in two other pictures, had this to say of the mother-daughter relationship: 'Shirley was the product of her mother. Shirley was the instrument on which her mother played. I don't know why the mother was like that – but I'd seen it before with Mary Pickford and her domineering mother. As a director, whenever I wanted anything from Shirley, I looked at the mother.' When 'Curly Top' showed any sign of flagging during her gruelling routine both on the set and off, her mother would call out: 'Sparkle, Shirley, sparkle!' and 'Dimples' would bravely snap back to attention.

The fact that Shirley fled into marriage at seventeen and would never hear of letting her own daughter become a child actress, (baby Temple Junior was actually offered a juicy five-year contract while still in the womb), says a lot about how she really felt regarding movie moms and the whole business of child stardom. In later years, still good-natured and still a trouper, she refrained from railing out against her mother and Hollywood, as many former child-stars were to do. But while still a child she had declared wistfully: 'I can't wait till I grow up. I don't exactly know why I want it so much. I think pehaps I have had enough of childhood. I think you have more fun when you grow up. I don't know why, but there is more. . . isn't there?' As pathetic a statement as any child could make, especially when that child happened to be the most photographed, one of the wealthiest, hailed as a genius, showered with gifts and drenched with affection.

Pretty, precocious and pert, Shirley Temple exerted a sort of magic that made her screen persona unreal, divorced from everyday care. But the burning question remains: can she really be classified as a movie nymphet, a Hollywood Lolita, however remotely and without meaning to be? To the original Temple fans, adults or children, the question would have seemed outrageous, as it was, indeed, when a similar question was asked even in Shirley's own day. Shirley Temple is alive and well and not yet retired from Republican politics, and so too is the person who had the temerity to raise the matter originally – the author Graham Greene. It resulted in a celebrated court case which Greene lost, which makes discussion of the matter delicate, even today. Nevertheless one should attempt to take a cautious peek at the problem.

For some reason, many otherwise normal human beings are charmed and amused by coquettish, even flirtatious behaviour on the part of young children, especially girls. They encourage it with applause, rewards and squeals of admiration. This fact was not lost on the moguls of Hollywood. The first thing they did when they started putting infants in movies was to make them mimic adult romance. In Hal Roach's *Our Gang* series, what most delighted adult audiences was childish imitation of courtship. In one 1935 episode for instance, seven-year-old Carl 'Alfalfa' Switzer wooed four-year-old Darla Hood by crooning, 'I'm in the mood for love.' Darla had to retire at the ripe old age of fourteen, just when she might really have started being interested in boys singing that sort of thing to her, but apparently no-one was interested any more in seeing her do that on a screen. What charmed audiences was the clever imitation, the caricature of grown-up behaviour. It was still prevalent in the seventies – who would have paid good money to see that banal gangster tale, *Bugsy Malone*, if the cheap tarts and hired killers it portrayed had been played by adults instead of children?

Shirley Temple began her career at the age of three in the *Baby Burlesks* series, which were very similar to the 'Our Gang' shorts. They featured toddlers but were aimed at adult audiences. These one-reelers were parodies of adult films and situations and often called for a tiny girl to make believe she was a big girl with sexually mature attributes and attitudes. In one of them, Shirley impersonated Marlene Dietrich – the reigning sex-symbol – suggestively rebaptized: 'The Incomparable More Legs Sweet Trick'. In another short called *Polly Tix in Washington*, she played a call-girl and sported black lace underwear. We see her in a still from this period garbed in a low-cut evening dress, vamping Baby Leroy with great know-how.

Something of the parodied sexiness imposed upon her by not overly scrupulous adults rubbed off on Shirley's manner and unwittingly remained with her during her early years. Her innocence and extreme youth would have made it impossible for her always to distinguish between a cheeky grin and a childish version of the cheesecake's c'mon, between a spoilt kid's pout and the 'bee-stung' pursed lips that prefigure the knowing kiss-kiss mouths of Marilyn Monroe or Brigitte Bardot. The fact that little Shirley was on the plump side and often wore exceedingly short skirts to make her look even younger than her real age, does occasionally give her a feminine cuteness that could be construed as mildly sensual. The fact that she was the star of all her films meant that the plot thus had to be constructed around her. Shirley usually played orphans, or at least motherless tykes. Her leading man might have a vague sweetheart or fiancee (indeed, he had gorgeous Carole Lombard in *Now and Forever*); but he had to spend most of his time with 'Miss Curly Top'. Audiences expected *her* to get maximum screen time.

When Shirley warbled away love songs like *The Right Somebody to Love*, *We Should be Together* or *When I'm With You*, they were usually sung *for* or *with* her leading man. This added to the slight ambiguity of her status: daughter-figure or precocious love interest? For every shot in which the little cutie kissed a lady, there were ten in which she hugged and kissed a desirable male. And when the leading man was as devastatingly handsome as Gary Cooper, every adult woman in the audience must have envied her when she nuzzled up to him. Of course, there wasn't a *soupçon* of sex in it; the man might well be playing the role of her father or grandfather (like Lionel Barrymore in *The Little Colonel*). Yet somehow this too fitted into the sentimental,

faintly incestuous dream so many little girls and adult women cherish of an idealized, 'us-only' relationship with an adoring father figure, preferably without serious competition from the big league of grown-up girls. Was it that quality of playing up to her adult leading men which led Gary Cooper to christen Shirley 'Wigglebritches'? The studios were careful to prevent that nick- name from getting wide publicity, suppos- edly fearing that 'Shirley's voluble following would, in part, take exception to such casual familiarity'. One wonders with whom one can be 'casually familiar' if not with a six- year-old one knows as well as Gary Cooper got to know the adoring 'Wigglebritches' during the long days they spent working and playing together during takes.

Left: *Shirley Temple ... one is seven, the other is seventy-seven, but we all know who's wrapping who around their little finger.* Below: *Shirley in* Wee Willie Winkie, *the film that got Graham Greene into big trouble.*

How far *did* Graham Greene go in his 1937 review of *Wee Willie Winkie* for the magazine *Night and Day* in suggesting that the attraction exerted by Shirley Temple might be sexually ambivalent? The answer is *too* far, since he was sued for libel and made to pay the then enormous sum of £2,000 to Shirley Temple herself, £1,000 to her film corporation and £500 to her film company. For obvious legal reasons, the review is no longer available for consultation and is not included in Greene's complete writings on films. Greene himself ruefully referred to it as 'the review which set 20th Century-Fox alight... Statement of claim – that I had accused 20th Century-Fox of "procuring" Miss Temple "for immoral purposes".' In the counsel's view, it was 'one of the most horrible libels that one could well imagine', 'a gross outrage,' and the magazine which had printed it such 'a beastly publication... that every respectable news distributor in London refused to be a party to selling it'. In

actual fact, *Night and Day* was a highbrow English equivalent of *The New Yorker*, with such already distinguished figures as Evelyn Waugh and Elizabeth Bowen on its regular staff. The scandalized language suggests a clash of interests, though a psychologist might counter that so hysterical a condemnation might, at least, conceal a private approval.

The nature of Greene's objection to the way Shirley Temple was used in films can be deduced from his 1936 review, in *The Spectator*, of *The Littlest Rebel*. In it, he spoke with distaste of 'the usual sentimental exploitation of childhood' and made an odd reference to the film's 'disreputable enjoyments'. He was even more explicit in another 1936 review for *The Spectator*, in which he more than hinted his conviction that Shirley Temple's success rested on a premature coquetry: 'The latest Shirley Temple picture is sentimental, a little depraved, with an appeal interestingly deca-

dent... Shirley Temple acts and dances with immense vigour and assurance, but some of her popularity seems to rest on a coquetry quite as mature as Miss [Claudette] Colbert's and an oddly precocious body as voluptuous in grey flannel trousers as Miss Dietrich's.' By this time, 20th Century-Fox must have been growling in its lair, though nine-year-old Shirley herself had no idea that such things were being written about her. It would be interesting to know what her opinion of the accusation was when she grew old enough to judge such matters. Would she at least concede, as Godfrey Winn wrote at the time about the libellous review that 'it was not a criticism of Shirley's clever acting at all, but one which introduced potential audience reactions – reactions which were entirely alien to Shirley's lovable and innocent humour.' Like Beauty, Lolita lies in the eye of the beholder. It is only the projection of Humbert's sick fantasy which turns her into an object of desire.

The whole issue was not Shirley Temple's obvious innocence, so much as some of her fans' – and her studio's – lack of it. As Greene had remarked in a review of a Deanna Durbin film, 'Innocence is a tricky subject: its appeal is not always quite so clean as a whistle.' Greene was pointing the finger at audience reactions and at the studios who catered for those audiences, not at the child performer herself. The case itself was soon buried and forgotten anyhow, along with the thirties' obsession with child stars. Yet it remains pertinent; indeed it is more relevant today than ever before, with film studios, directors and parents exploiting the nascent sex-appeal of girl children far more consciously and explicitly. Nobody cares now whether Temple's youthful appeal was uncalculatingly erotic or not. She is too sugar and spice for modern palates, and her films too kitsch for contemporary Humberts, raised on a meatier diet of foul-mouthed, cigarette-smoking Tatum O'Neal, nude Brooke Shields and bedroom-eyed Jodie Foster. The world has moved on.

Nevertheless, the question was tantalizingly raised in connection with Stanley Kubrick's *Lolita*. In his 1963 review of the film, critic Andrew Sarris had this to say of the leading lady: 'Sue Lyon .. although sexy, never approaches the intoxicating apricot innocence of Humbert's ultimate nymphet ... the buried prototype of Lolita, the true "creature of fantasy and desire" for the American culture, is Shirley Temple, who throughout her prepubescent movie career was paired off with adult males who loved her to distraction.

Where were you, Shirley Temple, when Sarris hinted that this hideous duo was possible? By 1963, nobody batted an eyelash at such a suggestion; most film critics agreed that the fifteen-year-old Sue Lyon looked far too old for the role of nymphet Lolita. It is safe to assume that any remake of *Lolita* will star a girl-child far younger than Sue Lyon. But it won't be Shirley Temple because there can never be another Shirley. 'God, he made her just all by herself. No series. Just one.'

sweethearts. Mary Pickford left the movies in 1932, the year Shirley Temple entered them.

JUDY GARLAND
A huge voice in a tiny body, the favourite
jazz baby of the thirties remained
something of a little girl lost
for the rest of her life

DEANNA DURBIN
'The little Diva', half-forgotten now, was
clever – and lucky – enough to become
'the one child star who grew
up to be happy'

ELIZABETH TAYLOR
The nymphet whose violet eyes and perfect
features allowed her to survive the
perilous jungle of puberty

4. Over The Rainbow
Lassie Come Home

By the time Shirley Temple was twelve, Templemania was dead. Wistfully, she sang in her last little-girl film (*Young People*, 1940): 'We're young people... We're not little babies anymore', in the forlorn hope that she would be accepted, even though she had cut off her baby curls and was sprouting little breasts. But America sulked. 'What's to become of Shirley Temple is one of the burning issues of the movie industry. She has lost some of her early prettiness and all of her babyish cuteness,' *Life* unkindly wrote, while a contemporary journalist, Leonard Hall, declared even more unkindly: 'America's Lollipop has become, alas, America's Pain in the Derrière.'

Temple's stardom was waning, yet the fashion for girls of a nymphet age was in full bloom. Deanna Durbin, Judy Garland and Elizabeth Taylor were all pubescent when their screen careers began to flourish: Deanna was just thirteen (and passing for younger), Judy was twelve, as was Elizabeth Taylor when she starred in the film that made her famous: *National Velvet*. How was it that they made the big time at the very age Shirley Temple was tactfully 'retired' by her mother? The answer is not difficult to find. Shirley's image was quintessentially cute, and such utter, unabashed cuteness is only becoming in a very young child. It palls in late childhood and appals in adolescence. All nymphets are cute by definition, but the teenage nymphets of the late thirties and early forties – Deanna Durbin, Elizabeth Taylor, Judy Garland, Gloria Jean and all the other Hollywood would-be's – could best be defined in their persona as 'sweet' rather than 'cute'. They were neither sexy nor provocative, nor naughty, but what the French would call 'gentille': wise virgins rather than foolish.

The sweetness of this new crop of Lolitas was not necessarily cloying and ineffective, though it was always pretty sentimental. These new nymphets were resourceful, like some of their predecessors; they portrayed damsels in distress who got on with the business of rescuing themselves without waiting for Prince Charming (or Humbert Humbert) to save them from whatever mess they found themselves in. Judy Garland tripping her way down the yellow brick road, ready for anything, is the figurehead of that generation of nymphets: prim and proper in her crisp, clean pinafore and her neat braids, polite and well-mannered, yet always quick to scold shams and bullies, she personified a no-nonsense approach to life that still left plenty of room for dreams and ideals. This bold approach nevertheless remained ladylike and decorous throughout; that very adult sense of convention, of right and wrong, of is and ought, was tempered by a childish ingenuousness and sense of wonder. Graham Greene, who had been so scathing about Shirley Temple, was more indulgent with this new crop of 'sweet' virgins; as he wrote of Deanna Durbin in his review of *First Love* (1939): 'There is nothing shabby or hypocritical in the dream which Miss Durbin expresses with the drive of irresistible conviction.' And though he was one of the few critics who disliked *The Wizard of Oz*, calling it 'an American drummer's dream of escape', he conceded that 'Miss Judy Garland, with her delectable long-legged stride, would have won one's heart for a whole winter season twenty years ago'.

If Greene thought he would have had to be twenty years younger for Judy Garland to win his heart, it was not to make the point that she could only appeal to a very young boy, but rather to excuse himself for being too European, too cynical and too world-

The Gumm Sisters (left to right: Frances, Sue and Virginia); the smallest of the three – soon to be known as Judy Garland – usually stole the show.

weary to appreciate the film and its heroine, as he makes clear in his review: 'To us in our old tribal continent, the morality seems a little crude and the fancy material rattles like dry goods'. But for men less urbane and sophisticated than Greene, girls like Garland, Durbin and Taylor had as much, if not more, appeal as they did for teenage boys.

Back in the thirties, film-going was by no means as dominated by younger audiences, as it has become more recently. The pubescent stars of many eighties 'brat-pack' movies (*Wargames*, *Back to the Future*, *Young Sherlock Holmes*, *About Last Night* and so on) are young only because the majority of movie-goers are under twenty-five. But in the thirties, when adults went just as ready as kids to see *Three Smart Girls*, *National Velvet* or *The Wizard of Oz*, men in their thirties, forties or much older were among the most avid fans and admirers of Deanna, Judy and Liz. It was their admiration which turned these little ladies into true Lolitas, however demure they were, both on and off-screen.

As Nabokov made it clear the whole concept of the nymphet exists in the covetous eye of an older man. Her teenage swain, on and off-screen, may see her as a love object, but not as a nymphet. Judy Garland, Deanna Durbin, Liz Taylor and Gloria Jean appealed not only to men old enough to be their fathers or grandfathers, but they were also often teamed up with male actors of more than a certain age, with whom they shared a reciprocal affection and intimacy. After all, under the make-up and the make-believe, it was three middle-aged men Judy was bossing around and fussing over in *The Wizard of Oz*. Elizabeth Taylor's true love was obviously her daddy in *Life with Father*. Gloria Jean's only well remembered film role was when she co-starred with crusty old W.C. Fields in *Never Give a Sucker an Even Break*. The title of one of Deanna Durbin's most successful films speaks for itself: *100 Men and a Girl*. As Marjorie Rosen put it in *Popcorn Venus*, in this film, Deanna spent her time 'marshalling a band of impotent men and dominatng them as moral conscience, mother, manager and promoter'.

Left: *Judy Garland and Deanna Durbin:
friendly rivals with sweet voices. Here the
'ragamuffin' meets the 'princess' in Judy's
first film* Every Sunday *Right· Margaret*

Those middle-aged men (and presumably those in the audiences who identified with them) seemed to revel in being bossed around by pretty young girls only half out of childhood. It was so much more appealing and less threatening than if a mature woman were doing the nagging, say the wife or – God forbid – the mother-in-law, both stock figures of fun and contempt in the film comedies of the thirties.

Judy Garland, Deanna Durbin and Elizabeth Taylor: three smart girls who embodied the wistful escapism of a difficult era. Each of them with their sweet faces and sweet voices, spunky yet feminine, was someone's favourite nymphet: a safe Lolita, who did not pose a threat to the sacred institution of marriage and the family (sexy Lolitas are notoriously lethal to both), who did not force red-blooded American males to question the nature of the feelings aroused in them, even when the sweet young things trilled their adult love-songs. When they grew up, these three smart girls had very different destinies, each exemplary in its way. And there was a fourth, not-so-smart girl – Gloria Jean – whose career was almost as meteorically successful as that of the other three, but whose adult destiny was the most sadly exemplary of all.

When Vincente Minelli worked with six-year-old Margaret O'Brien on *Meet Me In Saint Louis*, the child's mother (predictably another husbandless ex-dancer) serenely explained to the director how to make the little actress cry in the sad scenes; he just

64

*O'Brien and Judy Garland, two of the
cinema's best-loved nymphets. Both
sometimes needed something more than
gentle persuasion to perform.*

had to tell her that someone was about to kill her beloved puppy. If that wasn't enough, he would have to go into detail: how there would be blood everywhere, how the dog would suffer atrociously and yelp piteously for hours. It worked every time. Little Margaret O'Brien would soon start to shed buckets of beautiful tears as director and mother took turns whispering gruesome stories into her little ear. In his autobiography, Minelli admits that he 'felt like a monster' doing it, but did it anyway and got just the performance he wanted.

The star of *Meet Me In Saint Louis* was, of course, the young Judy Garland, whom the director married a few months later. When she had been a child stage-performer called Baby Gumm, her mother had used a similar trick to get the little girl to act on demand. At the least sign of un-cooperativeness, Ethel Gumm would threaten her youngest daughter (all of two when she started off) with abandonment. Judy never got over it. For the rest of her life, she manifested a pathological craving for reassurance and approval, but still could not assuage her original fear that she would be abandoned by those whose love she craved: husbands, lovers, fans, friends, children – if she proved unworthy.

'Somewhere Over The Rainbow' is, of course, the song with which Judy is most often associated. But when she was six or seven, her best solo performance as Baby Gumm was 'I Can't Give You Anything But Love' which she sang with startling maturity for such a tiny girl. It could have become her theme song – as it became Marilyn Monroe's, with whom she had in common the adult pathos born of a 'monstrous gilded solitude'. But fate decided otherwise and offered her 'Somewhere Over The Rainbow' – the song she so nearly never sang.

Between 'I Can't Give You Anything But Love' and 'Somewhere Over the Rainbow' lay ten years of growing up, of being

Left: *Judy Garland.* Below: *Louis B. Mayer with Judy and Mickey Rooney. He loved all his 'children' especially the young Judy. 'It's a pity she had to grow up,' he sighed on her twenty-first birthday.*

discovered, then forgotten, then discovered again. Ten years of name-changing, of place-changing, until she became once and forever Judy and the location was fixed on Hollywood. Born almost out of a trunk, (her father, mother and two older sisters were all vaudeville entertainers), Judy was stealing the show with her rendition of 'Jingle Bells' at age three. At first, the Gumm Sisters consisted only of the two older girls, with Baby Gumm making the odd appearance, but by the time Judy was five, she was part of the act and her shrewd mother must have grasped that here was the winner.

Now a trio, the Gumm sisters were one day mistakenly billed as the *Glumm* sisters, which sounded so depressing they decided to rechristen the whole lot as 'Garland'. A year later, Frances became Judy, and Judy it remained for the rest of her life, though the official surname changed five more times with five different husbands. It was clear to everyone by this time that Judy was incipient star material: she had the voice, the personality, the magic. What a shame she didn't have the looks! When someone asked Ethel Gumm why her daughter wasn't in movies, she replied – in Judy's presence – 'I guess she just isn't pretty enough.' Nevertheless, when the two older Gumm sisters went off to get married, Ethel Gumm concentrated her energies and ambition on her youngest offspring. She started touring Judy in vaudeville as a single performer. The child enjoyed the limelight and the applause, but her memories of Ethel during that period of her life are grim: 'My mother was truly a stage mother, a mean one. She would stand in the wings and if I didn't feel good she'd say "You go out there and sing or I'll wrap you round the bedpost and break you off short".' When displeased, she would lock up her daughter in their dingy hotel room, leaving her alone and terrified for hours on end. No wonder Judy's first reaction on learning of her father's death from meningitis was so tragic. 'Now,' she sobbed, 'there is no-one on my side.'

It was grimly appropriate that Judy's father should die just as she finally managed

Left: *Teenage Judy sandwiched between Jackie Coogan and Mickey Rooney. Judy was subjected to relentless grooming, massage and diet pills. These highly addictive drugs became a life-long habit.*

to land that coveted film contract with MGM studios. She thus found herself face to face with her mother at twelve – the peak Lolita age – at the very moment she was becoming a Hollywood nymphet: the fatal mother-daughter twosome, with Louis B. Mayer standing in for Humbert Humbert. There has been more than the usual amount of gossip about the true relationship between Judy and Mayer – a great fancier of young girls – and that gossip started when Judy was only fourteen. But as one biographer wrote: 'It must always remain in the area of speculation whether or not Mayer's intentions towards Judy were honorable and paternal, or neither.'

No-one, however, can deny Mayer's god-like influence on the young girl who, for the next seventeen years, 'worked, slept, ate, appeared in public, dated, married and divorced at his command'. All Ethel needed to get her way when she saw signs of rebellion in her teenage daughter was to say she'd tell Mr Mayer. When Judy turned twenty-one, Mayer is said to have sighed and

made a typically Humbertian statement: 'You know, it's too bad that she had to grow up.'

There are also several versions of how the twelve-year-old Judy was signed up by MGM in September 1935. The most common one is that she sang 'Zing! went the strings of my heart' for Mayer so feelingly that his heart strings vibrated equally harmoniously, and he offered her a contract on the spot without even a screen test. 'It was like discovering gold at Sutter's Creek. Mayer took her all over the lot that day and made her sing for everyone,' James Goode, an MGM executive, later recalled.

If there had been a preliminary screen test, Mayer might have hesitated. Would Judy's superb voice and lively, appealing personality make movie-goers forget that she was a pudgy, almost plain little girl with a turned-up nose, freckles and crooked teeth, too old to be a child star and not really cute enough for the nascent sex appeal of the nymphet type? Judy herself was horrified when she saw the preview of her first real part in a feature movie (*Pigskin Parade*, 1936). 'It was the most awful moment of my life,' she was to say. 'I thought I'd look as beautiful as Garbo or Crawford – that make-up and photography would automatically make me glamorous... I was frightful. I was fat – a fat little pig in pigtails.'

Another MGM executive saw it more objectively: 'On signing up Judy Garland, MGM have bought an extraordinary voice unfortunately attached to a mediocre body and a badly flawed face. In the next seven years, the voice would be trained, the teeth capped, the nose restructured, the thick waist held in by corsets and the body reshaped as well as possible by diet and massage.' This description succinctly sums up the relentless process of grooming that young girls were subjected to in the Hollywood of the thirties. It does not, however, suggest the emotional scarring and the psychological consequences of such methods on a sensitive child who was constantly being reminded of her unattractiveness at an age when even beauties feel insecure. Judy's family called her Monkey, or Pudge. Mayer himself fondly referred to her as 'My Little Hunchback'. A studio executive cheerily told her, 'You look like a monster', before putting her on a stringent reducing diet of chicken broth and amphetamines.

Those highly addictive drugs became a life-long habit, as did the powerful sleeping tablets she had to take to counter their effect at night. To some extent, Judy's incredible ebullience and gusto on screen in her early pictures can be attributed to the Dexedrine and Benzedrine she took in such hefty quantities. She was soon relying on them not only for slimming purposes but to fight off the recurring bouts of depression and anguish that became her life-long nightmare. She was sometimes so hopped up on stimulants when shooting a film that her future husband, Vincente Minelli, later recalled having to hold her down during a scene.

Judy's first screen test and one-reeler film, *Every Sunday*, were not calculated to reassure her about her looks: in both, she was teamed up with the conventionally

lovely Deanna Durbin. Judy described the scenes they did together as 'sort of Jazz versus Opera. I had an apple in my hand and a dirty face, and she was the Princess of Transylvania or some crazy thing.' Nevertheless, it was the vital, gutsy Judy MGM kept on, soon dropping the option on the lady-like, rather stiff Deanna; this showed that they had considerable faith in the future of their 'little hunchback', though letting go of Deanna proved a fantastic mistake: she was making a fortune for her new studio long before Judy became a star.

Though the sob-sisters later made much of Judy's teenage unhappiness, at the mercy of the studio executives and her steely mother, there were good – even great – moments as well as bad ones. Judy later blamed MGM and her mother for everything that had gone wrong with her, yet even she was ambivalent about that period of her life. 'Oh, the early days at MGM were a lot of laughs,' she would recall, adding ambiguously, 'It was all right if you were young and frightened – and we stayed frightened. Look

at us – Lana Turner, Elizabeth Taylor, Mickey Rooney, and me – we all came out of there a little ticky and kooky.' And they came out superstars, she might also have added, which was what these young people were programmed to want to be more than anything else in the world.

It was supremely ego-boosting for a little vaudeville performer to be signed up at $100 a week, going up to $1000 by her twentieth birthday, at a time when ten million Americans were out of work. 'Hey! I'm going to be a movie star!… I'll be going to school with Jackie Cooper and Freddie Bartholomew!' raved an ecstatic Judy when she signed her MGM contract. True, becoming a star also meant hearing herself coldly referred to as a 'property', and an 'investment'; producers thought nothing of summoning the growing girl to their office to ask her agonizing questions like, 'When is your next menstrual period and how far apart are they? Are they painful?' Assistant directors discussed her sprouting breasts disparagingly in her presence, complaining that they pointed in different directions and would have to be taped down. But becoming a star also meant being appreciated and admired by growing numbers of people who saw in her a lovable, warm human being as well as a talented young thing. Judy was easier to like than the more beautiful Elizabeth Taylor or Deanna Durbin. She made many lifelong friends during those early MGM years; one of the most important was Mickey Rooney, with whom she co-starred in a string of teenage pictures: *Thoroughbreds Don't Cry* (1937), *Love Finds Andy Hardy* (1938), *Babes In Arms* (1939), *Andy Hardy Meets Debutante* (1940) and *Life Begins For Andy Hardy* (1941). 'Mickey understood me,' Judy was to recall affectionately. 'He would tell me how to walk into a scene from off camera, the studio never bothered to tell me that, and he would suggest to me how to get the best out of a line.' According to Mickey: 'We just had to look at each other and we'd crack up. We knew instantly what we were both thinking.'

After a couple of years at MGM, Judy was a name but not quite a star. The apotheosis of her Hollywood Lolita career probably came on the fabled occasion when she was asked to sing a song specially composed for Clark Gable's thirty-sixth birthday, on February 1st, 1937. Judy was fourteen, passing for less, and was wearing a little dress with puffed sleeves that made her look younger than her age. With her big eyes, winsome face and tiny size (even as an adult, she was under five feet high), she by now looked the part of the movieland nymphet. She really did have a crush on Gable (since the age of twelve, she had had a succession of crushes on much older men), so it came quite naturally to her to sing the vapid words of 'Dear Mr Gable, you made me love you', half spoken, half sung, as she gazed at a photograph of her idol. 'Oh, gee, Mr Gable, I don't wanna bother you, but I am writing this to you… I just had to tell you about the time I saw you in *It Happened One Night*. That was the first time I ever saw you, and I knew right then that you were the nicest fellow in the world. I guess it was because you acted so – well, so natural-like, not like a real actor…'

The song was embarassingly sentimental and cloying. But little Judy already had that capacity very few singers have: to instill such conviction into silly words and an unexciting tune, such heart-searing emotion, that those foolish lines and notes turn into a minor masterpiece, a soul-shattering experience. The birthday audience and the King himself were overwhelmed. A misty-eyed Gable rushed up to her after the performance to hug and kiss her. This beautiful event made Judy burst into tears and there and then, a Star was Born.

It is generally agreed by film historians that it was Judy's repeat performance of 'Dear Mr Gable', slipped into *Broadway Melody of 1938* (1937) at the last minute, which really made her name familiar to the critics and the public. With that song, she stepped out of the ranks of the dozens of more or less anonymous child actors who milled about the Hollywood studios in the 1930s. She was now a name, a face and a voice, if not quite a star. That, of course, came with Judy's break into the big league –

with *The Wizard of Oz*, in 1939.

The choice of Judy for the leading role in *The Wizard of Oz* is now referred to as 'a piece of casting for which the whole world should be eternally grateful', but at the time MGM hoped to borrow the fabulously popular Shirley Temple from Fox for the part. Miles ahead of Judy in box-office terms, and of a much more suitable age, ten-year-old 'Miss Curly Top' was regarded as the obvious choice. The vastly successful Deanna Durbin was also considered for the part but, like Judy, she was considered a bit too nubile-looking. In the end, Judy won the day. She was already sixteen, but could be made up to look younger, and she had just the right sort of homespun, spontaneous personality to play a plucky little country girl from Kansas like Dorothy.

In *The Wizard of Oz*, Judy exemplified the child-woman ambivalence of the Hollywood Lolita, though in a non-sexy way. Is Dorothy a little girl or a very young woman? Or both? She has the pig-tails, the bobby-socks, the checked gingham dress, the naive manner and the scrubbed pink face of little girls; but she also has the developed figure (despite the 'love corsets' she wore!), the high-heeled pumps and the mature voice of one past childhood. Though Bert Lahr, Ray Bolger and Jack Haley (respectively the Cowardly Lion, the Tin Man and the Straw Man), towered over her in terms of size, age and experience, all regarded her as a sweet child. But the midgets who played the Munchkins treated her as a woman and were forever pinching her bottom and propositioning her.

This ambiguity about the child/woman status of Judy/Dorothy also explains why she nearly didn't get to sing 'Somewhere Over The Rainbow': the song was regarded as too old for a child to sing, and too old for the potential public of the movie. Mayer himself disliked it, thought it slowed down the action, and wanted it cut out. But associate producer, Arthur Freed, was so keen to keep it in that he braved the tyrant: 'The song stays – or I go,' he snarled. It stayed, and so did he.

'Over The Rainbow' made her just as much as she made the song. It became her signature tune for the rest of her life. As her biographer wrote, 'Even on the occasions when she had voice trouble, the audience preferred her to half-speak the words rather than for her not to perform it for them at all.' It could be said that Arthur Freed did her a great favour in holding on to the song, yet how much of a favour was it really? It's true that the seventeen-year-old Judy, rapidly growing up, soon to get married (she was engaged by her eighteenth birthday), won the special juvenile Academy Award for her performance in *The Wizard of Oz*. The 'pert and fresh-faced miss with the wonder-lit eyes of a believer in fairy-tales', as critic Frank Nugent described her Dorothy, was about to leave nymphet-land forever. Within a few short years, husband(s), child(ren), nervous breakdown(s), suicide attempt(s) and glittery vamp roles would stand between her present and the days when she had been the Hollywood Lolita of chaste but fervent daydreams. Yet something of the nymphet stardust still clung to the adult star;

*sleeves, a frilly collar and little curls tried
to make us forget what the dainty watch on
Deanna Durbin's wrist implacably
recorded: that time ticks fast for Hollywood
Lolitas, and soon runs out ...*

the face was no longer fresh, but the 'wonder-lit eyes of a believer in fairy-tales' continued to glow as they had in the rainbow days. Judy was very conscious of this when she said, many years later: 'I think the American people put their arms around me when I was a child performer, and they've kept them there – even when I was in trouble.'

In the 'little red schoolhouse' at MGM, two thirteen-year-old nymphets called Judy Garland and Deanna Durbin were taught music appreciation by a certain Miss McDonald. This lady was surprised to discover that 'jazz-baby' Judy loved classical music. 'Oh, much more than jazz,' she told her teacher, adding wistfully: 'But everybody says the money's in jazz.'

Deanna Durbin, who soon became Universal's 'little diva', proved Judy wrong. There was plenty of money to be made out of serious music in the Hollywood of the thirties, as long as it was movieland's soft-core version. It was music 'in the classical vein' rather than the hard stuff: Victorian ballads like 'Pale Hands I Loved', popular religious songs like 'Chapel Bells' or 'Ave Maria', Irving Berlin-style songs like 'Begin the Beguine', as well as the most popular of popular arias from operas like *La Traviata*.

Deanna was prim and proper, but she was a true Hollywood Lolita insofar as it was the contrast between what Graham Greene called her 'unaturally mature soprano voice' and her slender, girlish appearance that probably accounted for much of her success. She trilled away adult love-songs, yet wore white anklets and bows in her hair. As soon as she started looking too old for the ribbons and white socks, her fans lost interest in the voice, though it remained just as good. Once again it was the child-woman combination that had appealed to them. Deanna Durbin was to say many years later: 'Hollywood refused to let me grow up. Hollywood saw me as the eternal bobbysoxer.' Like Mary Pickford and Shirley Temple before her, she too was convinced that it was parents rather than their children who

were her real admirers, despite the Deanna Durbin dolls, dresses, ribbons and toys that were busily manufactured during her brief years of stardom. 'Just as the Hollywood-produced pin-up represents sex to many dissatisfied people, I represented an idealized daughter to the millions of frustrated fathers and mothers,' she would later reflect. And the idealized daughter of many a 'frustrated father' is one whose virginity is guaranteed by the ribbons and the white socks, while her singing holds out the promise of more mature sentimental delights.

Unlike Judy Garland, Deanna Durbin had not wanted to become a movie star, nor did she enjoy movie stardom. In 1935, she was a pretty twelve-year-old with a pretty voice who lived in Los Angeles with her unassuming middle-class family. She sang at church socials and had little-girl dreams of becoming an opera singer one day. But in that part of the world talent-scouts prowl wolf-like in their search for fresh young flesh, and Deanna was to be 'discovered',

singing 'Drink to me only with thine eyes' at a school recital. Far from being thrilled, Deanna was scared and reluctant to try her luck in the movies. When she went to the studio with her mother for a screen-test she is said to have broken down. 'I don't want to be an actress. You're all torturing me!' she sobbed.

Legend also has it that Mary Pickford, by then a director at Universal, gave Deanna her first real break: a role in a B-picture called *Three Smart Girls*. Little Mary always had an unerring eye for great potential cinema nymphets: after all, it was she who had introduced the pubescent Gish sisters to D.W. Griffith way back in 1915. Whatever it was that audiences wanted in a Hollywood Lolita, it was immediately apparent that Deanna Durbin had it. Over the next few years, the lovely little girl with the lovely big voice made a fortune for herself and for her studio; in 1947 she headed the US salary list. She did this by churning out two films a year which repeated the original formula of *Three Smart Girls* (1937): a sweet but shrewd young thing sorts out the problems

of those she encounters, breaking into song at regular intervals throughout the plot. *100 Men and a Girl* (1938), *Mad About Music* (1938), *That Certain Age* (1939), *Spring Parade* (1941), *Nice Girl* (1941), *His Butler's Sister* (1944) and many another creampuff concoction may have seemed imperishable in their day – one fan claimed to have seen *Mad About Music* 144 times – but none have withstood the test of time. Even the Mary Pickford and the Shirley Temple vehicles have fared better, and that is not saying much.

As we know, Deanna had not wanted to become a film actress. She did not much enjoy her career. A shy, retiring girl, she hated the gimmicky publicity that surrounded her and to which Shirley Temple, Judy Garland and Elizabeth Taylor readily lent themselves because it was part of the game. Signing autographs, being photographed hugging teddy-bears or in girl-scout uniforms, giving rigged-up interviews in which one spouted opinions in keeping with one's public image – she hated it all. She later summed up the destructive effect

of such an existence on a youngster, and what she had to say of her experience is applicable to almost every Hollywood Lolita of the twentieth century, as well as to all famous child actors in general: 'Fans took home an image of me and studio press agents filled in the personal details. They invented most of them and before I could resist, this worldwide picture of me came back stronger than the real person, and very often conflicted with it. How could a young, unformed girl fight this publicized image of herself while still groping for her own personality? I was a typical thirteen-year-old American girl. The character I was forced into had little or nothing in common with myself.'

Predictably, Deanna's fans were horrified when she tried to go beyond her sweet schoolgirlish image. An attempt to play a straight dramatic role was dismissed by critics as 'grotesque and outlandish'. Her first screen kiss caused a sensation in the press. And when it was rumoured that Deanna might be getting married, the gossip columnist Louella Parsons claimed that this item of news had caused more excitement and anguish at Universal than Hitler's march on Vienna. But Deanna went ahead with her plans and got married anyway while still in

*smiling — for a moment, one could see
what a very pretty mouth she had. The
tender dreamy gaze is also
uncharacteristic, but how becoming!*

her teens, exactly like her contemporaries, Shirley Temple, Judy Garland and Elizabeth Taylor. Early marriage reassures the ageing Hollywood Lolita, and while her fans, her studio and – usually – her mother make her feel that her individual merits cannot survive the baby years, at least one person in the world wants her to play a grown-up role: her husband. All these marriages broke up in each case after a year or two. The transition from adulated nymphet to responsible wife was too sudden.

But in Deanna's case, a second broken marriage did not prove too disastrous; nor did her fans' gradual loss of interest in her.

In fact, she later relished not being recognized in the street any more. By her midtwenties her film career was completely over; she left the country, refused nostalgia interviews and certainly meant it when she claimed to be much happier than in the heyday of her stardom. Deanna had always been a modest girl, but she could not resist boasting with quiet pride after returning to the anonymity she probably never should have left: 'I'm one child star who grew up to be happy.'

Stars are made in heaven, but would-be cinema nymphets are the stuff mother's

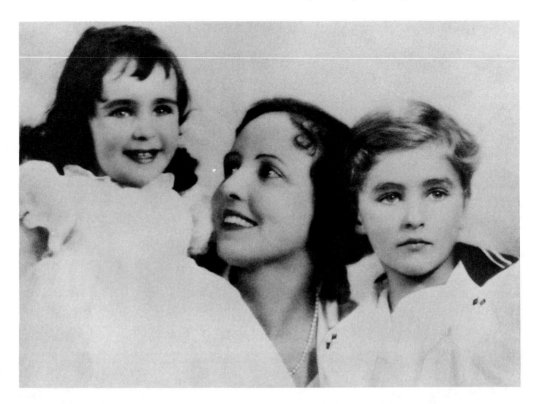

dreams are made of. Elizabeth Taylor had, to the nth degree, the three prerequisites for Hollywood Lolita stardom: she had a beautiful face, she was just the right age at the right time and, perhaps most important of all, she had a mother. As usual, the driving force behind Liz was a frustrated actress, described by one of her daughter's biographers as 'one of the most determined stage mothers ever to enter a casting director's office' – and that in a field where the competition for that sorry title is especially fierce.

Oh, she was a lady, Sara Taylor; she made much of her years in England, where Elizabeth was born, and the genteel existence they had led out there. Though she dreamt up most of the background of nannies wheeling great prams in Hyde Park and chauffeurs driving her little girl to tea at Buckingham Palace for the benefit of the studio publicity department, she wasn't really the brassy, pushy sort. But though her act was more discreet she was every bit as formidable as that of the vulgar, loud-mouthed mothers who openly exploited their children. Years later, the girl who stood in for Elizabeth (she wasn't called Liz in those days; her mother would never have allowed it), still recalled cringing inwardly each time she heard Sara's well-bred, piercing voice calling out 'Eli-zabeth!' on the film-set.

Sara Taylor had produced a child whose beauty could not be challenged, any more than Brooke Shields' could be a few decades later; she had also inculcated in that child the passionate desire to please mama that is characteristic of the true Hollywood Lolita. Mama lived to make her Elizabeth a star, and Elizabeth lived to fulfill her mother's expectation. The symbiosis was perfect: 'We think so alike it's as though we were the same person,' Sara once said of herself and her daughter.

The obsession with pleasing her mother, with avoiding anything that might displease her, had many advantages, but it also had one negative consequence. Elizabeth, like Brooke Shields later on, did not let go enough really to act for many years. Her presence on the screen was decorative in the extreme, but it was wooden. It was as though her soul were absent, as if she were the perfect doll-automat, wound up and remote-controlled by an invisible puppeteer. This was precisely the case.

The terror of displeasing mother may also have had something to do with Elizabeth's utter obsession with her appearance. Almost from infancy, Sara had so totally conditioned her daughter to live in fear of an awkward fold in her dress, a curl not quite in place, a scuff-mark on her shoe, that all the girl's energies were concentrated on avoiding such catastrophes.

She was born in 1932, with jet-black hair and deep blue eyes. The adoring public first met Elizabeth in 1943 in *Lassie Come Home*, her first big part and her first 'classic'. Generations of children since have cried their eyes out over the tribulations of Lassie. Generations of small boys have known their first pangs of passion upon seeing Elizabeth in her smart little coat and hat. Generations of small girls have known their first pangs of jealousy in the beautiful way Elizabeth's hair curled, at the way her eyes filled so becomingly with tears. The love and envy of one's subjects are the birthright of princesses, and Elizabeth has had far more than her fair share of both ever since she co-starred with a collie.

Hollywood-fashion, they had bought a whole lorry-load of collies for casting Lassie, from which they selected the most beautiful and docile, a one-year-old male dog called Pal. *Idem* for Elizabeth. As the film's producer, Samuel Marx, has described it: 'We had five other girls whom we were considering. We practically had selected one because I didn't expect much from Elizabeth. But the moment she entered there was a complete eclipse of all the others. She was stunning, dazzling.' The story goes that on the first day of shooting the cameraman asked the budding star to go back to the make-up man to have him remove an excess of mascara and eye-pencil. 'It isn't make-up. It's me,' Elizabeth apologized. And it was.

Pal did not have a mother to negotiate his contract, so he only cost the studio ten dollars. Elizabeth cost considerably more. Yet her part was much smaller than the collie's and of the two the dog was by far the more expressive actor. Reviewers raved about his performance, but of Elizabeth Taylor they only said that she was lovely to look at, which was undeniable. She had a long way to go: in her next film *Jane Eyre*, with two really pro child-actresses (Peggy Ann Garner and Margaret O'Brien) she didn't even rate a credit. In *The White Cliffs of Dover*, her next movie, her role was once again to look cute briefly while others got on with the real acting parts.

The young Elizabeth fared best when teamed up with animals. Was it because she liked them and thus came more to life in their company? Or was it because they brought her luck in her early career that she became a life-long animal lover? A film with a dog had made her face and name familiar to movie audiences. A film with a horse was to turn her into a star. Even though she now

played a butcher's daughter (a social come-down from the duke's grand-daughter she had been in *Lassie*), in *National Velvet*, Elizabeth won the child-star steeplechase by a mile. Never to grow more than sixty inches, (at least in height), she willed herself to grow three inches within three months to get the part. In the film, she co-starred with a gorgeous gelding named King Charles and with the very plebeian-looking Mickey Rooney, Judy Garland's old crony and co-star. *National Velvet* director Clarence Brown said of the twelve-year-old girl: 'There's something behind her eyes that you can't quite fathom. Something Garbo had.' He should have known: he had directed Garbo in no less than seven films. Did he mean mystery? Or soul? Or just a strange quality of absence? A star is a vessel into which we pour our dreams. There is a curious vacancy about Garbo's gaze, as there is about Elizabeth's, at least in all her early films. That emptiness leaves room for our fantasies. They nestle there and fill the beautiful void.

By her thirteenth birthday, the little princess found herself in possession of two horses, one her co-star King Charles, the other called Prince Charming. All three lived a royal existence that the real crown-princess Elizabeth, growing up in war-torn England, would probably have found most enviable. As Liz Taylor was to recall of those days: 'The star system was a golden, studio-protected cocoon. The people in it never smelled real life.' To its children, the studio was home, school and family. It was fame and fortune and ready access to screen gods called Clark Gable, Gary Cooper, Roy Rogers, Humphrey Bogart and all the others who reigned in movie Olympus. The golden cocoon protected one from all the knocks and shocks of life, so much so that, when Elizabeth's parents separated in 1946, she was unaffected. As she coolly recalled: 'It was no great loss. I had felt like an orphan for years. The ones I considered as my real father were my agent, Jules Goldstone, and Benny Thau, the head of artistic personnel at MGM. It was to them I turned for help and

advice.' For seventeen years, from *Lassie Come Home* (1942) to *Butterfield 8* (1960) MGM was Elizabeth's golden cocoon. During her brief nymphet years she gave interviews, posed with her many pets, wrote a much-publicized children's book about chipmunks and made another *Lassie* film: *The Courage of Lassie*. Animals still brought her luck in her career. As her biographer, Dick Sheppard, put it: 'With the exceptions of Richard Burton and Montgomery Clift, she never loved a co-star more convincingly than she did Lassie.' Long before she became Liz the Scarlet Woman, the Whore of Babylon, the husband stealer, the diamond collector, she was Elizabeth the virginal, the pure, the adorable and unattainable nymphet.

Lurking in the wings, watching over her as he did his other MGM nymphets was Humbert Humbert Louis B. Mayer, who, with real tears in his eyes, loved to repeat benignly to his little money-spinners: 'You are all my children and I am your father.' His solicitude did not prevent him from work-

ing himself up into towering rages when his 'daughters' – or their mothers – forgot their place and dared to challenge his decisions. On one occasion, when Sara Taylor questioned him about a forthcoming part for Elizabeth, he started foaming at the mouth (literally, not figuratively) and screamed: 'You and your daughter are nothing. Guttersnipes. I took you from the gutter and I can put you back there!' So much for the loving father. The twelve-year-old Elizabeth thus discovered early that golden cocoons are not necessarily the cosiest of places to live in, as Judy Garland and many another discovered before and after her. Of course, Elizabeth was too beautiful to need refashioning from top to toe as Judy had. But she could be ordered about, lent, sold, fired, blackballed and broken at will.

And indeed, for her next film Elizabeth was lent to Warner Brothers; in *Life With Father* (1947) she went from playing with puppies to playing with puppy-love. At fourteen, a peak age for Hollywood Lolitas, she was fast blooming into post-nymphet ma-

turity. Lolitas seemed to have gone out of style by the forties and yesterday's nymphets were in a tearing hurry to grow up, past the 'awkward age' in which they were too old for juveniles and too young for romantic leads. Physically, Elizabeth matured very rapidly. She had a large bust at an age when many girls are still as flat as boys. Perhaps she had willed it, as she had earlier willed herself into growing three inches. Her mother and studio helped to accelerate the process with almost indecent haste. Her very first date, arranged by MGM, was with a thirty-five-year-old studio escort, when she was only fourteen. Sara Taylor began to dress her daughter in low-cut black dresses so outrageously vampy that fan magazine readers complained. 'Why doesn't someone wise Elizabeth Taylor up?' one of them wrote, 'after all, she's only sixteen years old, but she dresses like she acts, like she is twenty or thirty.'

But Elizabeth too seemed in a hurry to grow up. When she was barely into her teens, one of the cameramen on the lot came up to her and said: 'I thought you'd like to know that the boys voted you the most beautiful woman they've ever photographed'. As soon as the man was out of sight, Elizabeth gasped: 'Mother, did you hear what he said? He called me a *woman!*' So goes life, particularly in Hollywood – the young girl's eagerness to break the bonds of childhood, to accede to the magic world of womanly privilege, soon turns into a life-long quest for lost youth, an endless nostalgia for the freshness and spontaneity, once so gladly discarded in the age of innocence. By the age of sixteen, Elizabeth looked 'about twenty-four' by her own reckoning, and was 'a full-blown sex-goddess'. She was playing the wife of thirty-seven-year-old Robert Taylor in *Conspirator* (1949), a role better suited to a woman ten years older than herself, and was being courted by the forty-four-year-old Howard Hughes. Outwardly, her nymphet days as chaste Elizabeth were over, but inwardly she was still an immature girl. The ambivalence of her position is apparent from her recollec-

tion of how she spent her time on the set of *Conspirator*, running from her leading man's passionate embraces to the childish business of doing her schoolwork. 'How,' she complained to her tutor, 'can I concentrate on my education when Robert Taylor keeps sticking his tongue down my throat?'

While she was still at that stage of her life – a fifteen to sixteen-year-old nymphet blooming into a sex goddess – Liz particularly attracted older men. Many celebrated figures courted her, attracted by her beauty as a budding woman rather than to her unripe charm as a nymphet. Both Orson Welles and Howard Hughes hovered round her for a time. Elizabeth, however, was no Lolita. She would probably much have preferred the attentions of boys her own age, but such youths were scared away by her very beauty and celebrity, let alone the shyness and reserve so apparent in all her early movie performances. At fourteen, she had begged her older brother, Howard, to help her meet boys. He is said to have replied: 'Get your own dates. You've got to

take chances like other girls. Call up a boy, get turned down maybe, like any other girl.' But neither Liz nor her brother's friends dared make the first move; and so, like countless more ordinary-looking girls of that age, she spent two or three anguished years feeling that maybe she was a freak of nature and that nobody would ever fall in love with her.

Her very early marriage to the young Nicky Hilton and her lasting infatuation with the equally youthful Montgomery Clift – her co-star in *A Place in the Sun* (1951) – put an end to her sexless-but-sexy teenage status. Although Clift was essentially homosexual, he seems to have reciprocated her love. By the time she was seventeen, Elizabeth had left nymphet-land for good. Gone forever were the days of her Lolita freshness, when she posed for publicity stills cuddling kittens and rabbits, her slender, immature, remote loveliness making the heart of every latent Humbert skip a beat. She had turned into a *femme fatale* in every sense of the word. From the naïve, unworldly girl-child of *National Velvet* to the sophisticated, spoilt beauty of *Julia Misbehaves*, the transition had been almost miraculously easy: a rare feat indeed in the history of Hollywood's nymphets, though not a unique one, since Natalie Wood also pulled it off a few years later.

Deanna Durbin sensibly chose to retire when it became apparent that she was more or less through in Hollywood terms. She had the good luck to find the right husband to tide her over the inevitable sufferings of the fallen star. After two false starts in life, the lassie came home to the waiting arms of a third husband in the French countryside. It is pleasant to think of her in the kitchen of her farmhouse, far from Hollywood hype, going into middle age in peace rather than in pieces, counting her blessings and her grandchildren, humming 'Pale Hands I Loved' – one of her standbys in her days of glory – as she makes *tarte aux pommes*. The neighbours overhear her as they pass in front of her kitchen window, and whisper

only half-believingly that plump, cosy Madame David was once the most highly paid female entertainer in the whole world!

How different, by comparison, was Judy Garland's post-nymphet existence: a long nightmare of neurosis, heartbreak, physical pain and addiction. But still, almost to the day of her death, she enjoyed the satisfaction of preserving the unswerving love and loyalty of her many fans, no small compensation for a born trouper. Bloated and broken, drunken and dazed, Judy's reputation flourished where others would have floundered forever. Artistically, she led a charmed existence. The more of a wreck she became, the more her looks seemed gone, the better her film performances. As a concert singer, she barely had to totter on stage and open her mouth to bring the house down. She'd be late, in tears, out of voice, but still Judy all the way, and thus even more adored. She had once and for all been identified with that little waif of a Dorothy bravely belting out 'Somewhere Over The Rainbow', tremulously querying why oh why she couldn't fly if the bluebirds did. After working her way through five husbands, as many pills as there are stars in

Left: *Elizabeth Taylor and Montgomery Clift in*
A Place in the Sun. *The film which put an
end to Elizabeth's teenage status and
turned her into a* femme fatale *oozing sex-
appeal.*

Heaven and enough booze to fill a good-size sea, Judy died at forty-seven. The coroner's verdict was 'accidental death from an incautious self-overdosage of sleeping-pills'. Charles Schram, her make-up man on *The Wizard of Oz* thirty years before, made up her corpse and fans sobbed that 'she'd found that rainbow now', even if the bluebird of happiness had forever eluded her. Judy paid a high price for becoming a myth in her lifetime, but myth she was and has remained, and that, after all, was perhaps what had mattered most to her all along.

Elizabeth Taylor's later career and love-life was also chequered to say the least, and the public – especially the press – was often cruel to her. Like Judy, she knew the misery of addiction, ill-health and broken marriages; her screen successes and the considerable critical acclaim she won in her post-Lassie years were probably a less vital need for her than they had been for Judy. One gets the impression, rightly or wrongly, that Liz was never all that ambitious *for herself*. As in her childhood she strove to

please her mother and her studio 'fathers', so perhaps in the Burton years it was more to impress her brilliant actor husband that she became a good actress. Anyway, Liz turned out to be pretty good at surviving both physical and emotional tribulations. Though she has so often been counted out – a casualty of the star system and of the film world's terrible pressure – she bounces back each time, having shed accumulated pounds and wrinkles. Inevitably there is a new sentimental interest to replace the irreplaceable *grand amour* of yesterday. To her dying day, she will fascinate and captivate, as much of a cult figure in her fifties as at fifteen. Hers may not have been the *good* life, but it seems to have been a lot of fun in spite of the knocks, and it also seems set to go on forever. In the year 2000, very probably, the *paparazzi* will still be popping their flashbulbs to light her passage, the grooms will still be fluttering about her at Maxim's, in a tizzy over Lizzy with the forever violet eyes. 'I'm Mother Courage', Liz once said; 'I'll be dragging my sable coat behind me into old age.' How delectably Hollywood-

ian is her concept of Brecht's Mother Courage in a sable coat! Liz takes obvious pride in being a survivor and claims to have written the epitaph she wants on her tomb:

HERE LIES ELIZABETH TAYLOR
THANK YOU FOR EVERY MOMENT
GOOD OR BAD.
I'VE ENJOYED IT ALL!

The unlucky one, the one. who got no compensation of any sort in her post-nymphet career, was Gloria Jean. Gloria *who*? It's a good question. 'Baby Schoonover' was the one who was slotted in to replace the ageing Deanna Durbin and Judy Garland. She was the one who was discovered by Joe Pasternak, producer of the early Durbin and Garland movies. She was the one with the perfect soprano voice, who sounded like Deanna; the one with the blue eyes and brown hair who looked like Deanna, who co-starred with Bing Crosby in *If I Had My Way* (1940) and with W.C. Fields in *Never*

Give A Sucker An Even Break. She was the one who starred in some twenty vehicles within a half a dozen years, then found all the studio doors slamming in her face when she reached the fatal age of seventeen-passing-for-fifteen, who thought she was going to be in movies 'all her life' and ended up as a restaurant waitress and receptionist to avoid going on welfare. She was the one who made pots of money for her studio, but whose own later earnings all went on back-taxes, so that she was completely broke by her mid-twenties.

Gloria Jean's story is the terrible tale of how Hollywood, the studio bosses and the public drop you when they no longer love or need you, when your capacity to lay those golden eggs comes to an end. What a debut it had been. At a time when the singing Lolita was still all the rage, she fitted the bill perfectly: so sweet-faced, so sweet-voiced, and above all so young, only ten when the fairy-tale began coming true, a good six years younger than the reigning musical nymphets, Judy Garland and Deanna Durbin. Hollywood, forever eager for fresh

*Gloria Jean, hailed as 'the next Deanna'
churned out film after film for six glorious
years until her studio dropped her
overnight and she faced years of obscurity.*

young blood, spared no pains in grooming 'Baby Schoonover' for stardom and in promoting its new wonder-girl.

Gloria Jean certainly had a smoother start than her elders, Judy and Deanna, who had paved the way for her: the yellow brick road was yellow because it was paved with pure gold. This was the lesson learnt at long last by those myopic studio bosses who had dropped Deanna's option and used Judy for nothing more than singing at birthday parties before wising up on her commercial potential. They wouldn't make the same mistake with Gloria Jean! The eleven-year-old starred in the very first movie she ever made (*The Under-Pup*, 1939), her name top-billed above that of Robert Cummings. But they did even better than that to promote the movie. 'The studio,' Gloria Jean recalled, 'chartered an entire train to take celebrities from Hollywood to Scranton, Pennsylvania [her home town] for the premier. 75,000 people turned out to meet the train, and I was the hometown girl who made good!'

From that time on, everyone was telling her she was to be 'the next Deanna', which she thought was the greatest compliment in the world. Of course, there was already a negative side to the coin. She was used to 'keep Miss Durbin in line' and perpetually hovered in the background as 'a potential replacement'. Not surprisingly, Gloria Jean found herself cold-shouldered by the older girl. 'Young as I was, I couldn't understand why she never spoke to me,' Gloria Jean wistfully remembered later. But success and adulation more than made up for Deanna's hostility. Pampered and groomed by Universal – who described her as 'Deanna Durbin's protégée' to a clucking press – she shared a schoolroom with Elizabeth Taylor, and churned out film after unmemorable film for half a dozen years with 'just about every star I had idolized'. The very titles of Gloria Jean vehicles have a forgettable ring: *A Little Bit of Heaven* (1941), *Wake Up And Dream* (1942), *Pardon My Rhythm* (1944), *I'll Remember April* (1945).

But Gloria Jean thought these films were all wonderful and that the 'fairy-tale come true' would last forever. What she was too young to assess during her half a dozen glorious years was that, unlike Elizabeth Taylor and Natalie Wood, her beauty was not outstanding. And unlike Judy Garland, her personality and singing talent were not so extraordinary that she could expect to make it over the hurdle of girlhood into adult stardom. Overnight her studio dropped her ('When I was rejected from Universal, it was like a relative had died. I couldn't even get on the lot without a pass, and no-one would give me one'). The pampered and spoilt seventeen-year-old from dreamland discovered the harsh realities of trying to sell herself to casting directors who dismissed her as 'too old to play ingenues and too baby-faced for more mature roles'. She discovered the harsh truth that nobody loves you when you're down and out, especially in Hollywood. 'When I looked up some of the people I had helped, you'd be amazed at the greeting I got. They thought I wanted a handout. This crushed me like you can't believe! I was absolutely heartbroken.' But there was still worse to come; when, almost destitute, Gloria Jean went to try and get a job, she discovered she was all but unemployable: 'What a frightening feeling... I had no qualifications for anything. I had been raised entirely "in the business", and now I was like a fish out of water. I couldn't type, for instance – and still can't. You see, I figured stardom would never end.'

Gloria Jean finally got a job as a restaurant hostess, then as a receptionist, and waited for twenty years, hoping against hope that she might get her second big break. The happiest legacy of a Hollywood upbringing may well be that faculty for believing there's always a somewhere over the rainbow, that if a dream came true once, an inconceivably exciting dream of glory and wealth for a little girl from Scranton, Pennsylvania, then it can – no, it must – come true again. Even in her forties, Gloria Jean was still confiding: 'I can still sing, I can still act... I'm still a ham at heart! I know I'm older and heavier... If I had a chance, though, I'd get myself in shape again. I sing just as well today, if not better.'

CARROLL BAKER
The first deliberately sexy movie
nymphet who enjoyed the
attentions of men but
made a game of
arousing
them

5. Baby is a Doll

Everyone loves a baby, but even more so when the object of all that affection isn't an infant at all. 'Baby' is the standard term of endearment applied by men to women of all ages who arouse feelings of tenderness and sexual desire in them. Every other popular song is addressed to a grown-up baby: 'Ah need my baby,' 'My baby and me,' 'Baby, come back to me,' 'Aw, please, baby' and so on. The ideal American baby has baby-blue eyes, baby-blonde hair and a baby's skin, but is just old enough to be handled in a very unbabyish fashion. In other words, she's a babe, a pretty baby, a baby vamp, a baby doll. When Carroll Baker went to Mississippi to star in Elia Kazan's *Baby Doll*, she discovered that it was the most common nickname around. Down in the deep south, it wasn't enough to be a man's baby: a baby *doll* was even more helpless, passive, dumb, and thus by definition cute.

How did fashion shift from thirties-style 'doll-baby' Shirley Temple to fifties-style 'Baby-Doll' Carroll Baker? Paradoxically, it may well have been the post-war Baby-boom of the late forties and early fifties which put an end to the delight Americans had taken in movies about children. With four or five kiddies of their own swarming about the house, the tired housewife and the bored father might be forgiven for preferring *Kismet* to *Bright Eyes* when they slipped off to their local drive-in. Perhaps, also, World War II had revealed too much for people to go on believing in good little fairies like Shirley Temple or Deanna Durbin who could get grown-ups out of the mess they'd got themselves into. Elizabeth Taylor might make the world safe for Lassie and her puppies, but not for democracy. Besides, photographs of children's expressions during the Blitz, the small, starved survivors of Auschwitz, the tiny Korean

orphan called 'the boy who never smiled', all made a mockery of those pre-war well-fed, grinning moppet saviours.

If there were few true Lolitas left on the screen in the late forties and early fifties, there were still several hopefuls about in Hollywood itself. Following the separate but parallel thread of Hollywood Humberts, Errol Flynn, the swashbuckling hero of many a movie epic, got involved in a succession of epic scandals with nymphets distinctly under the age of consent. The undeniably good-looking Flynn was permanently mobbed by female admirers, and often complained about being regarded as 'a male Mae West' who had to put on extraordinary sexual performances to live up to his reputation for virility. Perhaps he found very young girls less demanding in this respect, or perhaps he liked to do some of the chasing for a change; in any case, he got found out for the first time in 1942, when he was arrested and tried for statutory rape against two under-age girls. Again, as in the Chaplin case some fifteen years earlier, the double standard prevailed: had the girls in question been Deanna Durbin or Elizabeth Taylor, for example, it is quite likely that their careers would have been wrecked. But the trial actually helped to raise Flynn's box-office takings: audiences obviously wanted to see their swashbuckling hero in a new light. They were short-term gains however – he never really escaped his reputation as a lecher.

Defended by the best lawyers money could buy (the whole affair cost the actor $50,000, a huge sum in those days), Flynn was finally found 'not guilty' after a twenty-one day trial, on the grounds of 'insufficient evidence'. However, he had been skating on extremely thin ice, and he knew it. Afterwards, he admitted that he had had a plane

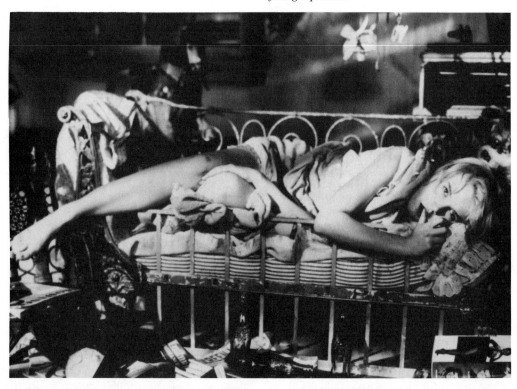

waiting for him to flee the country if he lost the case. As with Chaplin, the brutal exposure of his intimate life shook him deeply; he contemplated suicide and drank more heavily than ever before, a habit that would lead him to an early grave. Yet he had not learnt his lesson, any more than Chaplin did after the Mildred Harris scandal. Once a Humbert, always a Humbert. In 1950, Flynn was again involved in a statutory rape case with a fifteen-year-old girl. Though once again the charge was eventually dismissed, the American public was unsympathetic: Flynn was forty-one by this time, and had been remarried less than a month earlier – needless to say to a very much younger woman.

By the late fifties, Flynn was a complete wreck from alcohol and drugs; yet he had his last defiant fling with a retarded fifteen-year-old called Beverly Aadland, whom psychologists were to describe as 'emotionally closer to twelve or thirteen'. Though she lived with the fifty-year-old actor for the last two years of his life, Hollywood seemed to

have grown tired of prosecuting (and persecuting) Flynn for his taste in nymphets. It was only after his death that Beverly's mother, in the fine tradition of nymphets' mothers before and since, decided to cash in on the fact by writing a book entitled *The Beautiful Pervert*, which began as follows: 'My Beverly was only fifteen and still a virgin when she met Errol Flynn. A few hours later, she was still fifteen … but she wasn't a virgin any more.' The loving mother described in graphic detail the story of Flynn's affair with her 'baby', and her purple prose caused quite a sensation at the time. But by then Flynn was dead and the sixties had set in. The capacity for real-life Lolita-Humbert situations to shock had diminished – though it had by no means vanished, as Roman Polanski would discover to his cost quite a few years later.

The scarcity of screen nymphets in the late fifties did not herald the end of Hollywood Lolita – far from it. It would take her about a

to be cheered up and stimulated. Baby-doll just flopped about helplessly, sulked, pouted, got herself and others into a mess and was utterly dependent on her parent surrogates, especially upon her big sugar daddy, for economic support, pampering and cuddling. If she was at all smart, she kept quiet about it. The higher her IQ, the cleverer she was at concealing this dangerous fact. Doll-baby had been a woman in a child's body; baby-doll was a child in a woman's body. Both thus remained ambivalent in their appeal: woman-child and child-woman, the first physically asexual because she was so young, the second ambivalently sexy because she was so immature. Desiring her adult body made a man feel furtive and guilty for coveting a mere 'child'.

There were several categories of fifties baby-dolls apart from *the* Baby-doll so superbly embodied by Carroll Baker. These categories were different but complementary. They appealed to a variety of audiences, but they all had one thing in common: the new variety of Hollywood Lolita was once

decade – from 1948 to 1956 – to get her new image into focus, but in 1956, Carroll Baker emerged as the ultimate baby-doll. What was the difference between her and the doll-baby of the pre-war years? Doll-baby had been young in years, but shrewd and precocious. Baby-doll was older, but she was stupid and retarded. The secret of the doll-baby's cuteness had lain in the way she struck up grown-up poses, with a good sense, maturity and polish well beyond her age, whereas the baby-doll's appeal resided in her childishness, sometimes even baby-ishness. Baby-doll stared round-eyed at the world (Judy Holliday), spoke in a lisping baby voice (Marilyn Monroe), sucked her thumb and slept in a crib (Carroll Baker). Doll-baby got on with her life, defended cowardly lions, protected stupid straw men, helped shiftless relatives out of trouble if she wasn't an orphan and looked for adoptive parents if she was. She found jobs and wives for people, impersonated Ginger Rogers dancing or Al Jolson singing to entertain adults, who were always needing

again a grown-up nymphet acting out the Humbertian fantasy through her looks and her behaviour rather than by virtue of her chronological age. The prototype Hollywood Lolita of the silent screen had been a young girl pretending to be even younger than she was, often actually disguised as a child and playing child parts. She had mimicked the fancied innocence and purity of an idealized girl-child, chastely loved by the hero and drooled over by villainous Humberts. Hollywood Lolita of the thirties and early forties was a real-life little girl, often – but not always – actually younger than the Nabokovian nymphet, a cute little bundle of love and mischief involved with adults in all varieties of adult situations (work, war, crime, adventure) but never sexual ones.

One type of nymphet to emerge in the fifties was the *gamine*: wide-eyed, pixie-faced, her youthfulness so deliberately exaggerated that it was calculated to bring out incestuous-father longings in an adult male rather than straightforward boy-girl feelings of mutual attraction. To emphasize this nymphet's appeal, she was often teamed up with very much older men: Audrey Hepburn with the elderly Gary Cooper in *Love In The Afternoon*, Leslie Caron with the ageing Fred Astaire in *Daddy Long-Legs* (a role which had been played by the eight-year-old Shirley Temple in the thirties). The perverse charm of this variety of nymphet was that very childish-looking actresses were pretending a lack of experience and a sexual naïveté which their true age belied. Like Lillian Gish and Mary Pickford before them, Julie Harris in *Member Of The Wedding* and Mollie Perkins in *Anne Frank* were pretending to be twelve or thirteen-year-olds, wearing the dresses of twelve-year-olds, striking up twelve-year-old poses, yet with that mature aura about them which clearly stated a sexual awareness no twelve-year-old should have possessed. Given their real age, Leslie Caron's *Gigi* and Audrey Hepburn's *Sabrina* couldn't really have been so innocent in the ways of the world and of men. The resulting ambivalence (were audiences meant to want to pat these little girls on the head?) was perfectly conveyed by Maurice

Chevalier – himself an old Humbertian sophisticate – when he serenaded nubile Leslie Caron in his inimitably suggestive way at the end of *Gigi*: 'Thank Heaven for little girls'.

Leslie Caron, Pier Angeli, Audrey Hepburn, were fey, waif-like European Lolita types who made it big in Hollywood, but there were plenty of American gamines vying for the post of movie nymphet in the fifties. These were the cute dolls, the kind to whom a man would say admiringly: 'You're a real doll!' Debbie Reynolds, Shirley MacLaine and Doris Day all had 'the happy, freckled faces of childhood – still happy and freckled into maturity', as the author of *From Reverence to Rape* put it. But as Molly Haskel shrewdly added: 'Debbie Reynolds reminds one of a wretchedly precocious child who even at three was "the little lady", perfecting her dimples and dancing eyes for the day when they would come in handy.' Comparing a twenty-year-old to a three-year-old is less far-fetched than it might appear. So consummate was the art of those

monstrous nymphet, an overblown child. The adjectives 'innocent' and 'child-like' have been used almost as often for the grown-up Marilyn Monroe as for the infant Shirley Temple. In *Monkey Business*, one of Marilyn's early films, the hero (Cary Grant) hotly defends her irresponsible behaviour by asserting: 'She's half child.' To which his intellectually as well as physically mature girlfriend bitterly replies: 'Not the half which shows.'

If acting irresponsibly, being scatter-brained, silly and dependent are the pre-rogatives of extreme youth, then Marilyn was the biggest Lolita in the business, and her men the most fervid Humberts, revel-ling in – and exploiting – her supposed mental inferiority, her physical vulnerability (emphasized in her films by stiletto heels and/or extreme myopia) and her sheer inability to cope with existence unless there was a daddy figure constantly hovering in the wings. This was her stereotyped role in movies as it seems to have been in real life, not only with lovers but with friends and

latter-day nymphets, so perfectly juvenile their physique and mannerisms, that it really was difficult to distinguish Shirley Maclaine from her toddler daughter in a look-alike photograph of them which appeared on the cover of *Life* magazine. Doris Day was mocked for playing 'professional virgins' into her forties; but that cheery, freckled-faced virginity was a passport to never-ending pubescence – and work. Too 'young and innocent' for adult sexual involvement, she turned into a sort of geriatric case of Lolita in some of her later films.

These new Lolitas fulfilled one aspect of the American male's dream of eternal infan-tilism in his love object. But the sexy doll of the fifties – pneumatic, inflatable, brainless – fulfilled quite another. She was the fantasy of the little girl trapped in a big girl's body for the greater satisfaction of her mate. Outwardly, she seemed the opposite of the nymphet: big-bosomed, ripe-lipped, sophis-ticated in dress and manner, wobbling on stiletto heels, dripping with diamonds or longing to be. Yet she too was a sort of

acquaintances. Marilyn's bid for survival was to project the image of a little girl who has lost her way in the big department store of life, and who definitely won't make it unless *you* – the competent adult – take charge of her. So complete was her conviction that she was a helpless, irresponsible infant, that she made her appeal for indulgence and understanding even to other women: '*You*'re the grown-up, not me.' In her autobiography, Carroll Baker describes her rage not only at seeing Marilyn make a beeline for Carroll's husband and putting on her 'little girl act' with him for all she was worth, but also, to her amazement, doing it with her!

Theoretically, Lolita is under-age and thus not responsible for her actions. That is her strength as well as her weakness; she can literally get away with murder. In the sex war of the fifties, it was the ploy of many women, and Marilyn was their model, their figurehead: Lolita with big boobs, the adult nymphet who takes advantage of Humbert's oppression and obsession for her own pur-

poses. Yet the game is unequal; the Marilyn-style nymphet founders on the reef of economic or emotional dependence. There are no winners in Nabokov's original Lolita-Humbert duel since both of them ultimately die from having encountered one another. Many such duels end less dramatically, but Marilyn too lost out in the game of playing the eternal Lolita. She could not survive a Humbertless existence; right at the end, when her studio fired her, she was urged by friends to start a new life in Europe. She replied that she couldn't, not *on her own*; adults survive alone, not little girls.

Originally, Elia Kazan had hoped that Marilyn would play the role of Baby Doll in his film of Tennessee William's story. Marilyn – this was her Actor's Studio period – was keen to do so. That it didn't turn out that way is probably the best piece of cinematic luck since Pabst decided to use the little-known Louise Brooks instead of Marlene Dietrich as his leading lady in *Lulu*. For Carroll Baker created a new archetypal Nymphet in *Baby Doll*, as unique and dis-

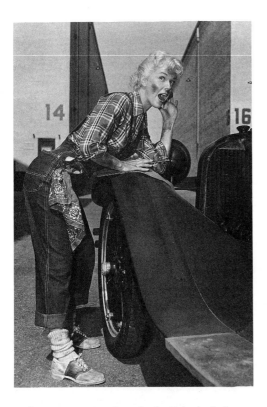

turbing as Louise Brooks in Pabst's *Lulu* or Lillian Gish as Nellie in Griffith's *Broken Blossoms*. Had she played Baby Doll, Marilyn would most likely have served up a rehash of her delicious sex-doll archetype, just as Marlene Dietrich could only have repeated her Blue Angel number in *Lulu*, a part she coveted. But Lola is no Lulu, and Sugar is no Baby-Doll. Just as Lulu had to be younger, more innocent and less worldly-wise than Lola, so Baby Doll imperatively had to be younger, less sophisticated and less of a professional vamp than gold-digging Lorelei Lee or the dim-witted but dazzling Cherie of *Bus Stop*.

Carroll Baker was perfect for the part. Marilyn pretending to be a Southern teen-aged virgin sleeping in a baby's crib and sucking her thumb would have been caricatural, almost grotesque. Carroll Baker made it seem quite natural, however absurd, and incredibly appealing. Through the little peephole bored in the wall by her lecherous husband, audiences of all ages turned into Dirty Old Humberts gloating at forbid-

den fruit. She wore her famous baby-doll pyjamas with the unselfconscious aplomb that little girls of a previous generation (Baby Peggy? Shirley Temple?) had worn very similar outfits: ultra-short dresses over matching rompers. In Marilyn, the retarded little-girl act always seemed just that – an act. In Carroll Baker, it came so naturally that it was forever after impossible to disassociate the actress from the maddening nymphet she played in the film. 'Baby Doll' became her middle name, and years later people in the street were asking her to suck her thumb for them. Round-faced, blank-eyed, open-mouthed and scruffy, she managed to look sexy in an *unknowing* way (Marilyn never forgot for a moment that she was sexy). A nymphet must be a bit knowing, but not too aware. Without Lolita's fundamental innocence, there is no vice to spur on Humbert's desire. Carroll Baker was totally believable as the mentally retarded, physically child-like, slightly overgrown nymphet, provocative yet passive, unkempt yet desirable, a doll to drive much older men mad (all the men in the film seem middle-aged; even Vacarro, the wily seducer who brings the doll somewhat to life, looks old enough to be her father. Clever Kazan knew better than to dim her nymphet's radiance by introducing a young chap her age, to whom she would not have been a nymphet).

Perhaps not surprisingly, *Baby Doll* was banned by the League of Decency and denounced from the pulpit by the omnipotent Cardinal Spellman of New York. Yet this was a story in which sexual intercourse did not occur a single time, in which nobody got undressed (unless one calls 'undress' in the literal sense of the word Baby Doll's rompers or the modest slip she wore later on), in which the most sex play that went on was a bit of stroking and tickling, with only one furtive kiss at the end between Carroll Baker and Eli Wallach. Compared with the explicit cinema sex of today this might seem small game, but it has been rightly said of movies made in the fifties that they were 'all about sex, but without sex'. Never was this truer than in *Baby Doll*. The film exudes sex, pulsates with sex, drips with it, floats away on it, explodes with it.

Wily old Cardinal Spellman was not taken in by protestations that nobody got Baby Doll in the end, that she started off and ended up a virgin in this tale of unconsummated marriage and unconsummated lust. Wily old Elia Kazan too admitted that he knew exactly what he was doing. In an interview, he declared: 'What I find erotic is amorous pursuit. To show the act itself is not erotic. What is erotic is "Will he or won't he get her?" And "Will she or won't she get him?" And how will they react? The arousal of desire is erotic, as well as the presence of desire before it is satisfied.'

Nor was wily little Carroll Baker taken in. She bluntly admitted feeling the electrically erotic climate which prevailed during the shooting of *Baby Doll*: 'In my efforts to be real in the sexually evocative scenes of the film, I worked myself into a combustible, near-volcanic state of desire. So much so that it wasn't all released on celluloid. I was still smouldering after the "takes", so that if anyone inadvertently touched me it was difficult to suppress a moan. I got really worried when I couldn't sit in the make-up chair without fear of climaxing ... it was that powder puff! ... or was I feeling an overwhelming lust for my make-up man? ... he caressed my face and earlobes and neck with that powder puff and drove me totally crazy!' She was so worked up by it all, she claimed, that she had to beg her husband to catch the first plane from New York to Mississippi to come and make love to her. Even this did not prevent her from acting like 'an over-imaginative overheated pubescent', as she herself put it. She described how, after the only kissing scene in the film, she forced her partner, Eli Wallach, to go on and on kissing her long after shooting had stopped: 'Although they had finished filming Eli and me kissing and had moved the camera away from us and into the kitchen set, I didn't release Eli... I just wouldn't stop kissing him. All through the lengthy dialogue between Milly and Karl, as well as several takes of that scene, I had Eli pinned against the outside wall of the set in an endless, inescapable kiss.'

If no coitus, implicit or explicit, was depicted in *Baby Doll*, then what was it that so shocked good Christians and so aroused Carroll Baker and later movie audiences? Nothing and everything. In the famous opening scene, we see balding, paunchy Karl Malden, the epitome of the seedy Humbertian Dirty Old Man, boring a hole (defloration symbol) in the wall to steal a glimpse of his unpossessed child-bride (voyeurism). He is on all fours (masochism) with a large dog by his side wagging its thick, curiously suggestive tail (echoes of zoophilia and auto-eroticism). Once the hole is bored, we catch a glimpse of Baby Doll asleep in a baby's cot (paedophilia) and sucking her thumb (symbolic fellatio). And this is only the brief first scene! How, except in terms of sexual symbolism, can one describe the way Baby Doll's husband, Archie Lee, brings her a drippingly phallic double ice-cream on a cone which she licks voluptuously while onlookers stare and snicker? Or the way her husband's enemy seduces her as he rocks her in a swing that simulates the slow, steady to-and-fro of intercourse? Or the way he teases and terrifies her by tickling her tummy with his fetishistic booted foot (he also wields a sadist's riding-crop much of the time)? Or the lip-licking sensuality with which they noisily munch their food as they gaze deep into each other's eyes towards the end?

With *Baby Doll*, Hollywood Lolita came of age, not because Carroll Baker was, technically-speaking, post-pubescent – in all other respects, she was a true nymphet – but because the film portrayed desire – not sex, desire – so explicitly and excitingly: the obsessive, almost criminal desire of a much older man for an elusive and hostile nymphet, then the arousal of her own desire by another man, an awakening which is like a symbolic puberty. It also portrayed a second older male, off-hand, condescending, paternal, who played with Baby Doll in an extremely sensual fashion, yet at the same time as he would have done with a little child, rocking her, teasing her, playing hide and seek with her, scaring her, making her laugh and cry at will, without ever taking her

Below: *Baby loves her dolly . . . but her daddy even more. She keeps his photo by her bedside and dreams of him at night. Carroll Baker in* Baby Doll.

seriously as a woman. One French film critic has described *Baby Doll* as the film 'which heralded and paved the way for *Lolita*, playing as vital a role as Nabokov's novel and *Playboy* magazine in the birth of the sexual revolution which America is going through today'.

So under his own terms, Cardinal Spellman of the Archdiocese of New York was quite right to single out the picture for special condemnation from the pulpit of Saint Patrick's Cathedral, calling on all good Catholics to stay away from the film 'under pain of sin'. This feeling was echoed by the Legion of Decency, which condemned the film as 'morally repellent both in theme and treatment' and reeking with 'carnal suggestiveness'. You bet. Catholic organizations across the country set up picket lines at theatres showing the movie, while some

But *Baby Doll* was not banned. It begot more baby-dolls, just as Carroll Baker begot a real-life baby-girl a few days after the film opened. The film was to spawn its own 'litter of Lolitas', each more forthright and explicit than the previous one, though none so artistic or sexy as the original. The symbol of *Baby Doll's* triumph over old-style mores and morality was beautiful: the famous/infamous picture of Baby Doll dressed in her rompers, curled up in her crib and sleepily sucking her thumb was painted on the largest Broadway billboard that Manhattan had ever seen – an entire city-block long! It taunted Cardinal Spellman on his return from Korea, where he had spent Christmas with the American soldiers posted over there. When he came back, he fumed from his pulpit: 'I went to see those boys who are risking their lives for their country and giving everything they've got to preserve our society, and when I come home, what do I find? *Baby Doll!*' That cry of anguish became a sign of the changing times. 'What do I find? *Baby Doll!*' was New York's in-joke of the year. To this day, no-one is certain that the good cardinal ever saw the film, but it is likely that, had they been given the choice, the boys out in Korea would rather have had a baby doll for Christmas than a cardinal.

Even so, *Baby Doll* did claim its own victims. It proved almost to be the kiss of death to Carroll Baker's career. Once a nymphet, always a nymphet in the public's eye, which is a problem long before the first crows feet start creeping across the temples. Carroll Baker ruefully admitted the fact at the end of her autobiography, inevitably entitled '*Baby Doll*' despite all her complaints at the way the label stuck to her over the years. 'That stupid little thumb-sucking brat is alive and well and seething still in the imagination of more than a generation of movie-goers,' she wrote. 'Oh, no thanks to me – for more than twenty-five years, I have devoted myself to her destruction. And I've grown so weary of the struggle, that my once maniacal resolve to eliminate her has gradually faded to a rather impotent wish. She, however, has retained every bit of her strength...'

bishops imposed a general economic boycott against the theatres where *Baby Doll* was playing. Certain extremists even threatened to plant bombs in those cinemas, justifying it to themselves within the framework of their old-style morality. They all sensed that *Baby Doll* was ushering in a new permissive age. Having gone this far, the cinema would have to go even further – a lot further.

TUESDAY WELD
The girl who didn't need to play Lolita on
the screen, because she played the
part in real life

SUE LYON
The nymphet who brought Nabokov's Lolita to
the screen and ruined her life
in the process

HAYLEY MILLS
Disneyland's version of the Hollywood screen
Lolita – innocent and carefree, but
perhaps sexy to some

CAROL LYNLEY
The twelve-year-old who got her kicks
through her well-filled
pocket-book

6. A Litter of Lolitas

Nabokov's Humbert Humbert had dreamed of the day his Lolita would spawn 'a litter of Lolitas', but at the end of the novel she died giving birth to a stillborn boy. The cinematic nymphet was however more successful. The Baby Doll of the fifties did indeed engender an assortment of movie Lolitas who all bore a definite resemblance to Carroll Baker: Tuesday Weld, Sue Lyon, Carol Lynley, Hayley Mills, and many another sixties' Hollywood hopeful. All were childish blondes in their early to late teens, with the vacant blue eyes of babies and the flawless porcelain complexion of dolls. The European child-woman type that was also becoming popular across the Atlantic (Brigitte Bardot, Sarah Miles, Françoise Dorleac, Jane Birkin, Catherine Deneuve and Julie Christie) were more sophisticated and knowing, but the fashion for baby vamps was worldwide, thanks in part to Nabokov's international bestseller.

The true nymphet, however, remained primarily American – blue-jeaned, gum-chewing and naïve. She was not sexually innocent, but innocent in terms of her age and culture (or lack of it). She was cute rather than beautiful. Beauty is a term for adult women, and she did not warrant that status. Her ideal of womanhood was the Barbie Doll, born round this time and with which all good little American girls played, the Barbie who – then as now – exemplified the American dream of femininity: slick, long-legged, smooth, platinum-haired and eternally young.

So alike were these baby Barbies, these ice cream-licking, hula-hooping Lolitas that it was often difficult to tell them apart: is that Carol Lynley in the photograph, or is it Carroll Baker? Is it Hayley Mills, Tuesday Weld, Sandra Dee or Sue Lyon? Hollywood too looked upon them as interchangeable:

both Lynley and Baker impersonated Jean Harlow on celluloid almost simultaneously. Tuesday Weld and Hayley Mills both claimed to have been offered the part of Stanley Kubrick's *Lolita* before Sue Lyon got it. These girls were as alike as puppies – or piglets – in the same litter, adorable clones who very briefly crystallized a certain ideal of the young girl, a bit dumb and depraved like their Baby Doll of a mother, yet cuddly and even wholesome in a cutie-pie manner that made the whole notion of sex possible with them in a way that would have been unthinkable back in the days of Lillian Gish, Miss Curly Top, Judy Garland and Deanna Durbin.

Loving Lolita had proved fatal for Humbert Humbert, but Lolita did not come unscathed through the experience either. Nabokov's Lolita had been in her prime at thirteen, still going strong at fourteen, rapidly declining by age fifteen and all washed-up by seventeen. A pretty, pampered, middle-class kid in the opening chapters of the novel, she turned into a deprived, proletarian housewife, unkempt and sluttish, in the closing chapter. The message could not have been more moral: sexual precocity is bad for little girls. Never accept candy from a stranger. You'll regret it later, and later is very soon.

The Hollywood Lolitas of the sixties all illustrated that very point to a greater or lesser degree in their lives: too much early success, too much early exposure to the glare of publicity, too much loose living at an age when good little girls should be fast asleep in their beds (preferably alone), wreaked terrible psychic damage on this batch of new-look nymphets. Nor were they luckier professionally than in their private lives: their considerable potential somehow never came to anything much, and their

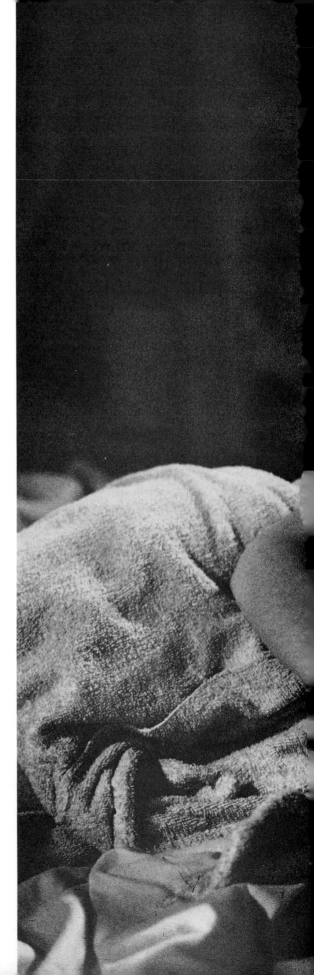

adult careers trailed off into the odd B-picture or television serial.

Earlier generations of movie nymphets had been exposed to enormous publicity and pressure by their studios – and their mothers – but they had also been rigorously sheltered from sexual exploitation both on screen and off. Their mothers were too keen to keep their babies babyish, and thus under their thumbs; old habits of obedience died hard: even when she was a married woman in her early twenties, Judy Garland announced her first pregnancy to her mother in a faltering voice: 'I'm going to have a baby, Ma. Do you mind?' As for the studios, they had invested too much in their 'property' to risk a scandal that might wreak havoc in their box-office returns. At seventeen, Elizabeth Taylor, Judy Garland and Deanna Durbin rarely had a proper date, and then it was usually chaperoned and organized by their studios!

A later generation of movie nymphets like Tatum O'Neal, Jodie Foster and Nastassia Kinski, would grow up in the days when sexual freedom and women's liberation had really started to mean something; more confident, readier to choose their partners, refusing to let themselves feel personally and professionally exploited even when the evidence pointed that way, some have apparently been less scarred when they emerged from their tearaway teens than the nymphets of the sixties. But the sixties Lolitas, like their older sisters of that same period, were an 'in-between' generation, unsure of itself; they hesitated between the security of fifties-style moral strictures and the emancipated seventies girl, who was ready to accept that solitude and pain might be the high price of independence and self-fulfilment. The sixties Lolita (significantly termed by the media, the 'dolly-bird') did not know where she stood: was she a sex-queen or was she a victim who had been sacrificed upon the altar of men's lust? Was she free when she had sex, got drunk, took drugs, or was she enslaved? Was she happy to attract so much attention (her very youth made her more newsworthy and blame-worthy than older actresses who over-

*The combination of a tender dreamy
childishness and a kind of eerie vulgarity
were essential requirements for Nabokov's
Lolita. Sue Lyon fitted the description
perfectly beating 800 other girls to the part.*

indulged)? Or was the glare of publicity driving her crazy? So much uncertainty turned her into a mixed-up kid who was so busy unravelling herself in her twenties that she was unable to concentrate on her career.

Otherwise, why didn't extremely talented teenaged actresses like Carol Lynley and Tuesday Weld become adult megastars? Why did Sue Lyon, whose ambition at sixteen was to become 'a cross between Brigitte Bardot and Marilyn Monroe', no less, become a cocktail waitress married to a life-convict instead? Why did Hayley Mills go off with a man of fifty when she was a Lolita-ish eighteen, and later end up as a believer in the Hare Krishna sect? Earlier film Lolitas had either been rejected out-of-hand by their public when they grew out of their little-girl status, or they had staunchly moved on to new and sometimes greater incarnations. The sixties generation of baby-blonde nymphets fizzled out, not with a bang but with a whimper.

'I didn't have to play Lolita, I *was* Lolita,' Tuesday Weld once declared. Was she boasting or confessing? In either case, she was only voicing an opinion of herself that everyone shared, approvingly or disapprovingly. For many years, no journalist ever wrote anything about her that did not include epithets such as 'archetypal nymphet', 'Shirley Temple with a leer', 'pubescent bad girl', 'teenage sex-kitten' or 'Bobby-soxer with a difference'. But Tuesday far outdid her literary model if we are to believe everything we read (and what she said of herself); her Hollywood version would have struck the novel's Lolita as really wild.

After all, Nabokov's Lolita was an ordinary kid until the age of twelve, and even after her sexual career began on the eve of her thirteenth birthday, she continued to go to school and do her homework. Hers was a monogamous relationship, and there was no question of orgiastic parties, hard liquor or even smoking, let alone using drugs. Tuesday, by her own admission, was having her first 'real affair' at eleven and was a

heavy drinker by age twelve. School was a dim memory – or rather a convenient excuse – by the time she entered her teens: 'I used to say I was going to school and head for [Greenwich] Village and get drunk instead.' As for drugs, 'I enjoy getting high on anything,' she was saying at a time it was still shocking to say such things. At fourteen, she was having an affair with her drinking buddy, 44-year-old Frank Sinatra, later married to Mia Farrow, who was herself once described as 'the thinking man's nymphet'. But Sinatra-Humbert was only one of a long line of Tuesday's lovers that included Albert Finney, John Barrymore, Terence Stamp and George Hamilton. 'Tuesday did some wild wild things and screwed up many many guys,' sighed Ryan O'Neal. She even tried running one of them down (actor Gary Lockwood) after an argument. The poor fellow had to jump up on to the bonnet of Tuesday's car and to plead for his life as she zoomed down Sunset Boulevard. But then perhaps she did not realize what she was doing at the time: 'I drank so much I can't remember anything,' she would say later, 'my teens passed by in drink.'

'Miss Weld is not a very good representative for the motion picture industry,' sniffed Louella Parsons in what was perhaps the only under-statement that good gossip-columnist ever made. Everyone was curiously indulgent towards the girl, probably because she was so obviously the archetypal movieland nymphet, as well as the first of an openly liberated breed whose representatives felt they had the right to play hooky, to go to all-night parties and to screw at thirteen, whatever the law and its old fogeys might say to the contrary. Such girls endeared themselves, not to everyone but to many, for their brand of tough-girl honesty and rueful cynicism is highly seductive in conjunction with an angelic face and a lithe young body. And then, of course, the poor kid had every excuse for going wrong: Tuesday, the archetypal nymphet, had had the archetypal Hollywood Lolita's childhood. Her father died when she was a toddler, and though she was the youngest in the family she soon became the sole bread-

claim. 'Modelling seemed such a glamorous world,' Tuesday admitted, 'what little girl wouldn't prefer it? You get out of school and before I was five I knew how to put on pancake make-up and lipstick. I lived out a little girl's fantasy of being grown-up.' Unfortunately, living out one's fantasy of being grown-up at five is not good for the psyche, as Tuesday's later psychiatrists, psychoanalysts and hypnotists must all have told her.

'I do not ever want to become a huge star,' Tuesday Weld once insisted. She got her wish. Not one of the films she played in can be called a classic. Most of them would hardly make it on the late show of a local TV. network. Four years before the sixties, she was already portraying a sixties nymphet at age thirteen in *Rock, Rock, Rock* (1956). As she herself put it: 'The girl I generally played was a little whorish teenager who would sleep with anybody, and yet has a childlike quality.' Her manner and her juvenile physique enabled her to go on playing that sort of role for another fifteen years, making her the oldest professional screen nymphet since Mary Pickford. When Tuesday was a kid, her off-screen goings-on were such that Danny Kaye described her as being 'fourteen, going on twenty-seven'. By 1970 he could have reversed the proposition, for she was still playing a convincing fourte-year-old at twenty-seven in *I Walk the Line*. Between her first and last Lolita roles were many pretty bad films in which she was pretty good: *Sex Kittens Go to College* (1960), *Wild in the Country* (1961), *Return to Peyton Place* (1961), *Bachelor Flat* (1963), *The Cincinnati Kid* (1965), *Lord Love a Duck* (1966), *Pretty Poison* (1968), among them. When she got too old for nymphet roles, her career trailed off into supporting roles and TV films.

Tuesday Weld later claimed to have been offered the leading role not only in *Lolita*, but also in *Bonnie and Clyde* and *Rosemary's Baby*. If she really turned them down, as she also claimed, she must have been the biggest masochist in the film business. Any one of those three films would have been her passport to cinematic

winner. When asked much later why she had broken off all contact with her mother in her mid-teens, she replied: 'If your mother sends you out to work as a model at the age of three, it is obvious why...' It was the usual story of maternal exploitation and, somewhere along the way, a sense of irremediable loss on the part of the child, an inborn feeling that one's right to love is bound up with one's earning capacities; the fact that one cannot define or rationalize such an impression at the age of four makes for even greater subsequent neurosis. Tuesday was precocious even in that respect: she had her first nervous breakdown at the age of nine, and made a suicide attempt at twelve.

But little Tuesday *enjoyed* being a child model, her mother would surely have maintained in her own self-defence; the mothers of Shirley Temple, Judy Garland, Jodie Foster and Brooke Shields, to name but a few, would doubtless have made the same

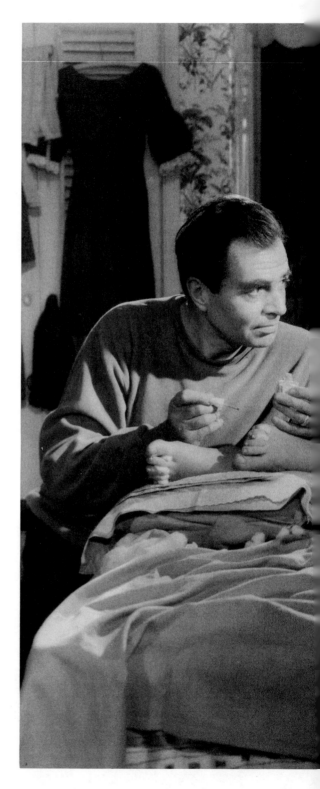

James Mason and Sue Lyon in Lolita. *Nonchalantly sipping a coke while an adoring 'dad' paints your toenails is perhaps every American woman's secret dream...*

eternity. Instead she became a footnote to the sixties, a half-remembered face and name in the limbo where all movie nymphets go after they grow up, unless some Humbertian movie-director has immortalized them in a film that will survive the passage of time. Tuesday Weld may have been Lolita in real life, but it was Sue Lyon who got the chance to be Lolita in the film version of the novel, a piece of luck which – as is often the case – both made and demolished her.

It can be safely claimed that Stanley Kubrick saved Sue Lyon from nymphet limbo when he made her his *Lolita* in 1962. Both she and the film were much decried at the time, but both are well on the way to critical rehabilitation twenty-five years later.

The primary objection made at the time to Sue Lyon playing Lolita was that she was too old at fourteen; but the novel covered five years of Lolita's life, from twelve to seventeen. If the film was to tell the whole story from Humbert's first vision of the young girl, lying pristine in the sunshine, 'a gaspingly adorable pubescent pet', to his very last glimpse of her, frumpy and hugely pregnant, the movie nymphet would have to be at the half-way age of fourteen to fifteen. It would have been more ridiculous to expect a twelve-year-old actress to impersonate a married mother-to-be at the end than to expect a ripe girl of fourteen to play an under-developed pre-teen nymphet at the beginning. Using two different actresses would have been unsatisfactory, as it always is.

Yet it was as essential to the film as it was to the novel that we *should* see Lolita from Humbert Humbert's first to his last glance of her: to realize, as he did, the irremediable harm he had wreaked on her young life, and also to realize, as he did, that despite 'her ruined looks and her adult, rope-veined narrow hands and her goose-flesh white arms, and her shallow ears and her unkempt armpits ... hopelessly worn at seventeen,' it was still 'love at first sight, at last sight, at ever and ever sight.' Even the 'old' Sue Lyon

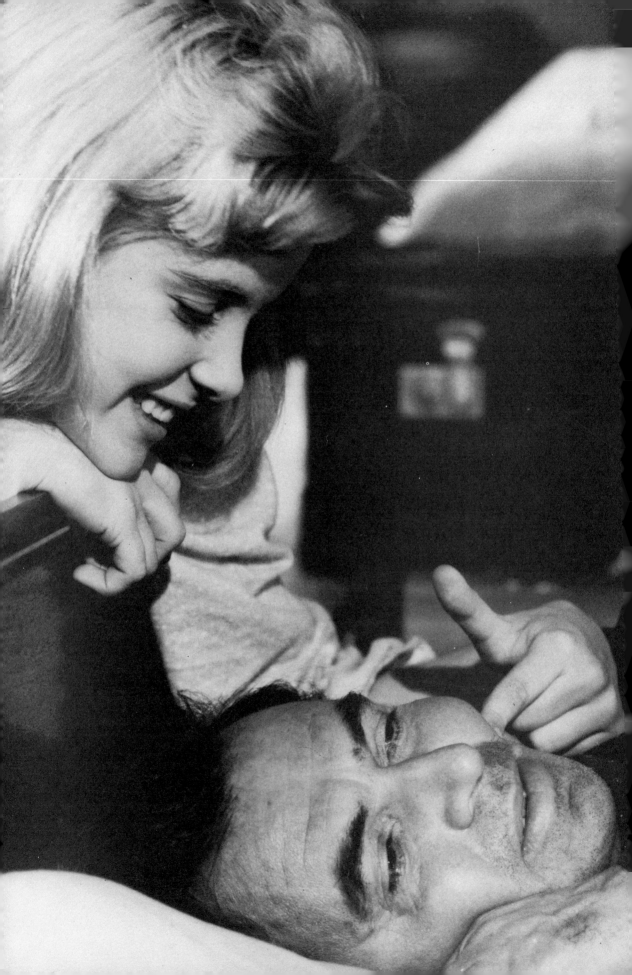

found it difficult to look the part of this final
Lolita. Had she been only six months
younger, it would have been impossible.

The real problem wasn't that Sue Lyon
was too old to play Lolita, but that people
thought she dressed and acted too old for
the part. She looked too cool and sophisticated in her high-heeled shoes and carefully
curled hair. Too womanly and knowing in
her cinch-belts and full skirts. But after all,
that was how little girls dressed in the fifties
when they went to the Prom at their Junior
High. In his dinner jacket and his fur-
collared overcoat, James Mason also looked
older than his age in the novel, which was
forty. And Sue Lyon, with her round face and
vacant eyes looked barely out of childhood.
Above all, she had a quality much emphasized by Nabokov as vital to a nymphet's
appeal: 'A tender dreamy childishness and a
kind of eerie vulgarity, stemming from the
snub-nosed cuteness of ads and magazine
pictures ... radiant, relaxed, caressing me
with her tender, mysterious, impure,
indifferent, twilight eyes – for all the world,
like the cheapest of cheap cuties. For that is
what nymphets imitate.' Those who had not
read the book (and they included little Sue
Lyon, who tried but found it 'too involved'
for her and gave up) did not register the fact
that Lolita, like Sue, also wore flaked nail-
varnish on her stubby fingers, smudged
lipstick, and spoke in a twangy, nasal voice
that might seem unattractive to a 'normal'
male, but which Humbert Humbert found
irresistible.

Kubrick had not chosen Sue Lyon at
random. On the contrary: he and MGM
producer James B. Harris had interviewed
some eight hundred applicants to play what
has been termed 'the most sought-after
juvenile role in history'. Unable to find *the*
Lolita of Lolitas among professionals and
unknowns, he had all but decided to post-
pone the scheduled start of shooting. Then
he saw Sue Lyon. She was appearing on The
Loretta Young Show on TV, and he immediately arranged a screen test. In it he found
the combination of 'dreamy childishness'
and 'eerie vulgarity' he was looking for, and
signed her up for seven years. A true

daughter of thumb-sucking Baby Doll, Sue
Lyon's childish vulgarity was less studied,
more spontaneous than the much older
Carroll Baker's. She gazed upon poor Humbert Humbert's adult passion for her with
just the right mixture of curiosity and
amused distaste, gradually turning into hostility and disgust. She was both seductress
and victim, Barbie-cool and baby-scared
when confronted with a man's dangerous
lust for her immature charms.

When her later life became an awesome
mess, Sue Lyon bitterly complained that 'my
destruction as a person dates from that
movie [*Lolita*]'. She made a good case for
her allegation, and one that must strike an
echo in many another Hollywood Lolita,
past, present and future: 'I defy any pretty
girl who is rocketed to world stardom at
fifteen in a sex-nymphet role to stay on a
level path thereafter.' She went on to explain the all-too predictable pitfalls: 'Overnight exposure to fame, money, handsome
actors and endless parties is, shall we say,
liable to blow you off course... I laughed off
all the warnings, but they were absolutely
right. *Lolita* exposed me to temptations no
girl of that age should undergo.' Stanley
Kubrick might have been overcome with
remorse, as Humbert Humbert was in the
novel, if all the responsibility for wrecking
Sue Lyon's young life had truly lain with
him. The facts of the case were a little more
complicated, however, although they did
not emerge until much later. Originally, the
details of Sue Lyon's pre-*Lolita* existence
had been ordinary enough, but they fitted in
perfectly with the classic movie-nymphet
pattern: Sue was the youngest of a family of
five, and her father died when she was ten
months old. The family moved to Los
Angeles when Sue was small, and what little
money there had been soon ran out. Attempts to turn the child into a breadwinner
did not start until relatively late, and Sue was
a cute twelve-year-old before it was decided
that she might have a future selling her
looks. At that age, like the novel's Lolita, she
was 'a disgustingly conventional little girl',
who liked pop music, dancing, going to
movies and eating gooey concoctions at

drugstores. This was the official picture, the image she projected of herself when interviewers began to take an interest in her. 'Not a Lolita. Not an innocent baby either,' she told them, 'just an ordinary, typical sort of grown-up American girl ... that's all.' She was also quick to insist at an early stage, 'No, being Lolita hasn't changed my life in any way. Why should it? I'm just the same...'

Ten years later, however, Sue Lyon described her whole childhood as 'a confusion'. Did she exaggerate its ugliness to excuse her adult disasters, as she had previously exaggerated her 'ordinary, typical' background? The new version was stark, to say the least. Sue now told interviewers that her mean, selfish mother had driven her father to suicide, later becoming both a drug addict and an alcoholic and marrying a succession of awful men. She had goaded her youngest daughter into a movie career, in the hope that the child would be her passport to a higher living standard. Miserably poor, they had taken a lodger into their run-down house. The lodger had tried to

rape eight-year-old Sue at knife-point and the case had been taken to court, but the man got off. At twelve, Sue had dyed her mousey hair blonde and had gone to work as a model. Like Lolita, she had had her first affair on the eve of her thirteenth birthday.

Like Lolita, Sue Lyon married at seventeen because she was starved of love (she had left home and mother as soon as she started earning enough as an actress). Less than a year later, she found her husband in bed with another girl and got a divorce. She then remarried, to a black football-player, and had a child by him. This was in the sixties, when racism was still rife in the United States (Martin Luther King was assassinated in 1967), and Sue felt obliged to leave the country and move to Spain. None of this was helpful to her acting career, though she had received very good reviews for her parts in *The Night of the Iguana* (1964) and *Tony Rome* (1967). A definitely self-destructive life-pattern was emerging. Instead of trying to make her difficult marriage work, she made her husband acutely

jealous by starting a long, increasingly torrid correspondence with a soldier in Vietnam, to whom she ultimately got engaged, and with a convicted murderer serving a forty-year gaol sentence, whom she met after her second divorce and her return to the United States.

When she first visited her sinister pen-pal, 'Cotton' Adamson, at the Canon Penitentiary, she felt 'a love so bizarre, so inexplicable that no-one could have predicted it'. She described his appearance as 'negligible', yet she also found him 'an incredible man with dazzling charm'; they were soon married, in 1973, though the marriage could not be consummated, and Sue Lyon went to live in a motel just by the penitentiary. The story intrigued newspaper columnists for a time, but scared away any remaining film producers; Sue Lyon's film and TV career had petered out almost completely by the time she was twenty-five.

In spite of his baroque imagination, Nabokov himself could not have thought up an odder, more haunting end for *his* Lolita. He could well have left the reader with that last vision of ruined youth and promise: a pretty blonde sitting alone with her young baby in a dingy motel room by a roaring highway in some god-forsaken corner of America, with a window view of a penitentiary watch-tower profiled against a bleak, empty sky, and going out to work as a cocktail waitress in the evening to pay for her motel. The novel's Lolita also spent most of her nights with Humbert Humbert in seedy motels, just as she too ended up working in highway restaurants for a living. Oscar Wilde was right to say that nature imitates art.

But neither literature nor real life are perfect: Nabokov made his heroine die in childbirth, a hackneyed literary device. And the real Sue Lyon eventually grew tired of that existence and filed for divorce on the grounds that her marriage had 'irretrievably broken down'. 'Where are you hiding, Dolores Haze?... Where are you riding, Dolores Haze?... Who is your hero, Dolores Haze?...' were some of the questions Humbert Humbert asked in a poem he wrote after Lolita had vanished from his life. For the forty-year-old Sue Lyon, the actual celluloid Lolita, the answer is drab. She is 'hiding' as a lower middle-class housewife, in a nondescript middle-western town, hating the movies and musing on her back porch about how *Lolita* ruined her life.

'The most talented youngster to be seen on the screen since Deanna Durbin, Margaret O'Brien and Shirley Temple'; 'The universal daughter of the sixties, a sort of Virgin Mary Pickford'; 'World star'; 'a veritable genius and the first real successor of the spun-sugar crown of Shirley Temple'; 'the wunderkind'; 'The golden girl of British films'; 'Actress of the year at sixteen'; 'Everyone's favourite daughter, little sister, girl next door or – for those with more bizarre interests – Lolita symbol'. Who on earth were all these reviewers raving about? Well, for those who were around in the sixties, it's pretty obvious: Hayley Mills, of course. Who else?

For those who weren't around at the time, it might not be so easy to come up with the answer. The most successful, most popular, most internationally acclaimed pup from the sixties litter of Lolitas has until very recently also suffered from the 'Whatever happened to...' syndrome. Her brief, dazzling, juvenile career followed the all-too predictable movie nymphet pattern: overnight celebrity, mega-exposure in the media, a frenetic period of churning out starring vehicles, never fast enough for adoring fans, a concentration of adulation, hard work, unreality and astronomic earnings, encapsulated within a few brief years, then a slow, at first barely noticeable decline as the years set in, a quiet but steady loss of returns at the box-office, increasing difficulty in finding suitable parts ('Too old for juveniles, too young for romantic leads, my dear'), acceptance of roles that one would have rejected out of hand in films that one would have considered beneath one's status a very short time before. And, one day, the discovery that one has become a pretty young actress out of a very large number of others for casting directors to choose from;

Hayley Mills and Maurice Chevalier, still thanking heaven for little girls: Hollywood's youngest leading lady and oldest leading man joined forces in In Search of the Castaways.

one has a name and reputation, of course, but one's juvenile stardom can be a disadvantage rather than an advantage; audiences want new faces, or else they have retained a stereotyped image dear to their heart which they refuse to relinquish. Their nostalgic memory of an adorable moppet, a coy nymph, an innocent tomboy or a virginal maiden, does not tally with this new vision of young womanhood showing off a sexy figure to best advantage and pursing her nubile lips for some serious screen kissing.

'Hayley is still a child … but she is growing up so very fast … I think she will, picture after picture, turn into one of England's most popular, most attractive female stars,' 74-year-old Maurice Chevalier predicted when he co-starred with fifteen-year-old Hayley in Disney's *In Search of the Castaways* (1963). But the problem was that when Hayley Mills *did* turn into an attractive, talented adult actress, people were still coming up to her fifteen years later, not to tell her how good or beautiful she had become with age, but how many times they had seen *Castaways* and other sugar and spice epics she had starred in when she was a nymphet.

Was Hayley Mills a movie nymphet, or a true Hollywood Lolita for that matter? Some of the vital ingredients were there and some were not. To begin with, she was English and the daughter of a quintessentially British actor, Sir John Mills. However she went to Hollywood at thirteen and she had just the right American-style looks that are a Humbert Humbert's delight: blonde, snub-nosed, knobbly-kneed, tomboyish and gracefully gawky in a happy, coltish way. No-one could say that she looked sexually precocious or knowing in the manner of a Sue Lyon or a Tuesday Weld; yet her very first film, *Tiger Bay* (1959) was a somewhat ambiguous adventure story about a twelve-year-old girl and a murderer. She held his fate in her hands, but was curiously drawn to him and, instead of denouncing him to the police, befriended and protected him, not so much out of compassion or kind-heartedness but because it was clear that the little slum kid on the verge of pubescence was not indifferent to handsome Horst Buchholz's animal magnetism. Much of the film's success rested on the ambivalent complicity that bound the girl child and the male adult, very reminiscent of that which existed in a beautiful French film of that same period: *Les Dimanches de Ville d'Avray.*

It was not, however, Hayley's nascent sex-appeal that was subsequently exploited after her personal triumph in *Tiger Bay.* Unlike many another Hollywood Lolita, she came from a family which had no financial need to emphasize that side of their growing daughter's personality. On the other hand it was a 'showbiz' family with inevitable movie contacts, so it was natural for Hayley to have a go, especially with her looks. In Hollywood, however, she was snapped up by Walt Disney Studios, which offered a 100 per cent guarantee of Pickfordian sweetness and innocence. Indeed Hayley's very first film for Disney was a remake of *Pollyanna* (1960), the sunny-tempered, pig-tailed darling who brought gladness to the hearts of all. She won a special Oscar for her performance and, before long, her name was regularly appearing on the list of the Ten Top Box Office Stars. The slight moral ambiguities of *Tiger Bay* were forgotten. Hayley had become a bubbly, asexual, wholesomely cute Baby Doll in all her Disney and Disney-style films: *The Parent Trap* (1961), *In Search of the Castaways* (1963), *The Moon Spinners* (1963), *The Truth about Spring* (1964), *That Darn Cat* (1965), *The Trouble with Angels* (1965), and *Sky West and Crooked* (1965). Hayley became a family institution. Mothers named their babies after her. You could safely take your kids to any film she appeared in.

Yet something in her must have appealed not only to the kiddies and to the clucking mamas in the audience, but also to the Dirty Old Men lurking within some respectable and other not-so-respectable males. Most people at the time would have scoffed at the notion that Hayley could be regarded as a sexy nymphet, yet the fact remains that she was very seriously considered for the coveted role of Lolita. She

had to refuse, because it would have completely spoilt her wholesome Disney image; but, ironically, whereas Sue Lyon later claimed that playing Lolita had ruined her life, Hayley Mills regretted having turned down the part, feeling it might have helped her to grow up both in her personal life and in her acting career. 'I might not have had such a difficult time growing up if I had accepted,' she later explained.

Tuesday Weld and Sue Lyon found it hard going to be propelled into a sexy nymphet's real-life role at the tender age of fifteen. Hayley Mills found it just as hard to grow up with the Pollyanna, 'everybody's favourite daughter' label sticking to her wherever she went. Towards her seventeenth birthday, she sank into a deep depression, that eventually verged on clinical breakdown. She kept repeating: 'My mind is dead. I'm like a big brown donut with a hole in the middle.' She was going through the all-too familiar pangs of the ageing Hollywood nymphet who feels that nobody wants her to grow up, just when a girl most needs to be encouraged in that direction; the terror that no one will even *like* her any more if she gets any older, that she is letting down her fans, her studio, often her mother, and all the people who have made her what she is rapidly ceasing to be: a child star.

'I was struggling for so long with the little girl image,' Hayley later recalled. 'I seemed doomed forever to be a little girl, whatever I did. And I knew nobody wanted me to change anyway.' The mildest attempt to appear more mature and self-confident was instantly squashed: 'There was a hell of a stink if I was seen with a cigarette, and no pictures were allowed to be taken of me holding a glass just in case someone thought the drink might be alcoholic.' She became morbidly self-conscious: 'I always thought people expected more of me than I could give and that I would he a huge disappointment to them. So at every party I went to I spent the whole time hiding in the loo.' She was even more ill-at-ease with youngsters of her own age, feeling they would make fun of her for being different or for being so far behind them academically: 'I was scared stiff

who converted her to the Hare Krishna sect: 'They have found something that they know will never go,' she explained blissfully. 'What he and the movement have taught me has made me a much wiser, kinder, person. I can now cope with my difficulties and disappointments and problems.' Was one of those disappointments the fact that Hayley's career, impeded by her hang-ups and her checkered private life, had tapered down from mega-stardom to quiet TV serials, even though in her portrayal of the English mother in *The Flame Trees of Thika* (1981) she was well-received as a serious actress in her own right. She shared that fate with all the other sixties Lolitas, and like almost all movie nymphets before her, she was to declare: 'I should never let any children of mine go into it... Of course, you have a marvellous time when you're doing it all, but you end up completely uneducated.'

of other teenagers.' Her strict work routine and dawn departures for the studio made it almost impossible for her to date boys, but when she did, as her mother recalled: 'It was difficult for her to tell whether a boy liked her for herself or simply because she was Hayley Mills.'

Though it shocked and astounded every-one at the time, it was not really surprising that Hayley, at a very immature eighteen, should have sought security and under-standing in the arms of 52-year-old Roy Boulting, who had produced *The Family Way* (1966), the first, rather coy, film to try to portray her as an adult. When she finally married Boulting, her parents were not the only ones to be horrified: enraged young men all over the world wrote her violent letters accusing her of setting a bad example for youth. But Hayley did not find the serenity and maturity she always felt eluded her, not with Boulting, nor with her second husband, a man of her own age. She may have felt that she had found it at last with a man fourteen years younger than herself

Carol Lynley was another sixties Hollywood Lolita who, like Hayley Mills, played virginal nymphets in Disney movies as well as unwholesome (ie sexually experienced) nymphets like Sue Lyon and Tuesday Weld, who was a childhood pal of hers. Less famous than the other three, she was just as perfect a specimen of the Baby Doll litter: round-faced and healthy, cute rather than beautiful, with cornflower-blue eyes and cornflake-coloured hair. 'An all-American candy-floss kid, a cream-puff cutie,' as Anne Leslie described her. Like all American nym-phets, she had a tendency 'to reach for a lollipop when I get depressed', and, by her own admission, she was also 'hooked on coffee ice-cream'. Small wonder that this comestible darling first acted in a play called *Under the Yum Yum Tree*!

Once again, hers was the typical Holly-wood Lolita's background. Born Carolyn Lee, she became a child model to support her broke and single mother; while working hard for a living at the lollipop-licking age, she was also trying to 'be a mother to her mother', as she later put it, adding ruefully: 'But I didn't make a very good job of her.

She was a trial … we were hopeless for one another.' Carol also happened to be a good actress. So good that at fifteen she was starring – now as Carol Lynley – in Broadway plays; when she showed up in Hollywood the same year (1958), she was gushingly described as 'the brightest thing the movies have seen for a long time', and even as 'the most important young actress to come along since Elizabeth Taylor'.

She became a 'Disney Girl' with *The Light in the Forest* (1958) and *Holiday for Lovers* (1959), but gave her finest performance as a juvenile playing a disturbed, sexually aware young teenager in *Blue Jeans* (1959). The childish sexuality of Jean Harlow seems to have been a must for those who handled their sixties 'blonde bombshell' successors, and like Carroll Baker, Carol Lynley was cast in the title role in a made-for-TV movie in the same year as Baker's version, 1966.

Later, she made a successful move into mature roles with Otto Preminger's *Bunny Lake is Missing* (1965) but she never made it to major stardom, and also followed the predictable Hollywood nymphet pattern of marriage at eighteen and divorce at twenty-one.

Carol Lynley was one of the few Hollywood Lolitas to admit frankly her keen interest in the financial rewards attendant on selling one's nubile charms. 'Where the money goes, I go,' little Carol coolly declared at the tender age of thirteen. And, looking back on those early years of quick money, she confessed that lollipops were not her only way out of depression: 'If I got depressed, I'd get out my bank book and gaze at it and it made me feel happy again.' Most other movie nymphets have not been so honest, sidestepping the issue and making light of the fact that their infant careers made them very well-heeled as well as very mixed up, a compensation of sorts. Even the profit-hungry Carol was true to the Hollywood Lolita credo, however, when she declared long after she had grown up: 'As for my youth, I have no regrets. But let me say I wouldn't want to do it again.'

LINDA BLAIR
Possessed by the Devil on screen, she soon
became possessed herself by drugs,
the FBI and murderous maniacs

TATUM O'NEAL
The seventies-style baby-nymphet,
foul-mouthed, cigar-smoking,
forever Daddy's girl

NASTASSIA KINSKI
Roman Polanski's ideal nymphet,
whose sexual power has never
been surprising . . .

7. To the Devil, a Daughter

The Devil has always had many daughters, and they have grown more daemonic as the years have passed. In a sense, Lolita is always something of a devil's child, even against her will. She lures, however innocently, grown men into forbidden paths that can lead to eternal damnation in the next world and to jail, disgrace and remorse in this one. She is Lilith, the forbidden fruit, doubly forbidden because unripe; and once tasted she can poison a whole existence.

It has been said that the obsession with the movie nymphet reflects America's ambivalence towards its youth: an ambivalence made up of fear and desire. No other country is so preoccupied with its teen and even pre-teen culture, so eager to imitate it, so quick to condemn it, to make a sort of religion of the very fact of being young, or, failing that, of trying to look and act young. Nymphets are the high priestesses of this cult, girls who can give to adult males the illusion that they have not yet left the paradise of youth. For some reason – perhaps more anthropological than socio-cultural – the male nymphet, or 'faun', to use Nabokov's term, does not have the same impact on grown women: the cute little boys of the screen have inspired a less ambivalent, maternal adoration in their lady fans, though doubtless some have been the secret darlings of male homosexuals.

The odd thing is that the grown woman, whatever her age, often *identifies* with the movie nymphet, becomes that irresistible baby seductress who always gets her way and manipulates men at will. This explains why so many of Mary Pickford's, Shirley Temple's, or Deanna Durbin's fans were women, not jealous of their little idols' screen persona and success, since it became *their* success for the space of an hour or two. By virtue of their charm, energy and talent these very young girls achieved sensational results that few mature women could ever have hoped for themselves in real life.

But Mary Pickford, Shirley Temple and Deanna Durbin were innocent nymphets, who got their way in a man's world without resorting to sex. They weren't above flirting or using coy feminine wiles, but theirs was an angelic, not a devilish power. The in-between nymphets of the fifties and sixties might be more sexually aware and manipulative, but that was because they were older and shrewder, and *using* their nymphet power, which in their case meant virginity and a childish appearance (think of Debbie Reynolds, Leslie Caron or Audrey Hepburn). The really young, and sometimes not so young, nymphets who tried using sex as a weapon still usually ended up as the victims even though they thought they had the winning ticket at first: Carroll Baker's Baby Doll was cunningly exploited by Eli Wallach, in Elia Kazan's film. Tuesday Weld got raped by her evil step-father in *Peyton Place*. Sue Lyon came to a bad end for having played grown-up games too young. Carol Lynley was an unmarried pregnant teenager in *Blue Jeans*, a fate worse than death back in those days. Only Hayley Mills joyously pursued the tradition of the daisy-picking nymphet who had graced Hollywood movie tradition since its inception: the golden-curled virgin so innocent that she doesn't know what the word virgin means, let alone what evil lurks in the dark wood beyond the sunny glade where she weaves that endless daisy-chain.

But the Devil knows that professional film temptresses are often no match for a posy of nymphets, especially in a world where it grows harder and harder to be truly shocking. The late sixties and early seventies were the years of Sexual Liberation, of Anything Goes, of Pornography For The Masses. Anybody can see scenes of seduction and fornication in close-up and Technicolor every day, even in family-rated films like the *James Bond* or *Indiana Jones* series. Familiarity, in the words of the old cliché, breeds contempt or at least acquiescence. The decadent Roman crowds who used to watch ladies copulating with asses at their local amphitheatres must also have stifled a yawn or two: when you've seen one, you've seen them all ...

What about the nymphet in all this? She is, by definition, *young*. Youth is, by definition, *innocent* and its wilful corruption is still taboo. In our jaded Western societies, freshness still startles, still holds promise, still excites. We are not talking here of the perverts, of the true paedophiles who get a kick out of 'chicken porn' – the lurid visual representation, live, on video or in photographs, of little kids having sex with adults. We are talking of the great mass of adults who, having left their tender years far behind them, are sentimentally moved by the recollection of youth when they see it depicted on a screen. They are often disappointed with real life and with their real-life partner, and they recall with yearning that in-between age when all was still possible, still potential, when the bud was turning into bloom and the dew was fresh on the petal.

But as the years passed and Hollywood 'came of age', the overt sexual appeal of the movie nymphet came creeping out of the closet. The nymphet inspired desires that were not always repressed, and she was sometimes an accomplice, a partner in crime, as well as a victim. And the seventies and eighties have introduced uglier, more discordant notes: child prostitution in *Taxi-Driver* (1976) and *Pretty Baby* (1978), possession by the forces of evil in *The Exorcist* (1974) or *To the Devil a Daughter* (1976), incest in European films like *Beau-Père* and *Charlotte Forever* (1986). The uncomfortable and sordid underside of the movie nymphet phenomenon probably culminated in *Streetwise* (1983), a full-length documentary about Tiny, a *real* thirteen-year-old child prostitute and her cronies, *really* at work, not in some distant, poverty stricken Third World country, nor even in decadent, old world Europe, but in the good old U.S. of A.

The ugly face of the Lolita cult in Hollywood first erupted in the seventies in the person of Linda Blair, gruesome nymphet heroine of a gruesome smash hit: *The Exorcist* (1974). Though Linda's performance was obviously effective, mostly thanks to horrendous special effects and gallons of greenish bile, she vanished too soon from sight to be more than a precursor – an omen even as one of the *Exorcist* sequels was called, of things to come. Linda obviously had talent – she was nominated for an Oscar for her performance as a demented child possessed by the Devil but was finally outclassed by the even more youthful Tatum O'Neal – but the movie proved to be the kiss of death to her, as well as the kiss of the demon. Although, bizarrely enough, there was talk soon afterwards that she should star in the remake of *National Velvet*, she never managed to pull away from the horror factory. Indeed after the shock effects and the obscenities of *The Exorcist*, the gentle role of Velvet made famous by Elizabeth Taylor seemed tame to fourteen-year-old Linda: 'I don't like that story very much,' she poo-poohed to an interviewer, 'It's a little old-fashioned.'

Linda's story is interesting only insofar as it exemplified once again the Hollywood Lolita syndrome at its most classic. She too had been 'working for a living' since the age of six, making commercials, before *The Exorcist* shot her to rather unsavoury international fame. She suddenly became a face people recognized in the street; she signed autographs, posed for photographers and spoke about her household pets. Both she and her mother hotly insisted that becoming a celebrity had not changed little Linda one bit: she was still a normal American schoolgirl, looking and dressing the part of the wholesome movie nymphet, with her round baby cheeks, her long straight hair, her jeans and her suede jacket, and her big big smile, especially if there was a camera handy.

Then, once again in the most classical Hollywood Lolita pattern, the dream gradually turned to nightmare and the story got grimmer and grimmer, though it did not emerge until a few years later. At twenty-two, Linda was to admit that her teenage fame had plunged her into a sordid world of sex and drugs, saying: 'I grew up fast. I've had more relationships than some people 40 or 50 years old.' She described how growing up in Hollywood 'burnt people out', felt that this had happened to her too and that she had been 'pushed into a lot of situations' no youngster should have been pushed into. At fifteen she had already left home to live with TV actor Rick Springfield, whom she left for a married man at sixteen. Gradually, her own teenage years turned into something of a horror movie: promiscuity, drugs, threats from crazed fans who developed a sick obsession about her after seeing *The Exorcist*. At one stage, there she was, still a little teenage nymphet, having to hide both from the FBI, hot on her trail in connection 'with a drug-peddling ring, and from some mad gunman who claimed to have already killed one actor', and who believed Linda was 'A Devil-possessed nymphomaniac'. Such threats could not be taken lightly: Hollywood was still reeling at the memory of the Sharon Tate murders, and it would not be too long before another crazy almost succeeded in assassinating President Reagan because of his obsession with another movie nymphet: Jodie Foster.

Instead of being sent to prison for 'conspiring to possess cocaine', Linda Blair was finally put on three years' probation; as part of the court's penalty she had to make public appearances warning against the danger of using drugs. She might, as a personal touch, have added a few words about the dangers of appearing in horror movies in one's early teens and becoming yet another over-exposed, over-extended Hollywood Lolita.

While Linda Blair's puppy fat cheeks spilled green bile into the front row of the stalls, the world was also experiencing an incredible craze for a funny little female urchin called Tatum O'Neal. Aged all of nine, she starred in *Paper Moon* (1973) with her father Ryan O'Neal, hero of an earlier smash hit: *Love Story*. *Paper Moon* was film buff Peter Bogdanovich's revamped seventies version of the old-style tragi-comedy that had made kiddies like Shirley Temple and Jane Withers famous and it is full of coy references to silent movies of the time in which the film is set. A little orphaned tyke teams up with an at-first reluctant adult male, in this case a con-man on the run, they become inseparable and live through a series of wild adventures before the bittersweet happy ending.

In her denim overalls and her funny hat, with her round face and short tousled hair, Tatum O'Neal looked like Jackie Coogan in *The Kid*, where he also helped his father-substitute Chaplin to earn an illicit living for them both by breaking the windows Charlie then replaced. But as Tatum was a girl, she was inevitably compared to Shirley Temple by almost every critic, who raved that she was the hottest property to surface in the film world since 'Miss Curly Top'. This is said routinely every time a new female child star appears on the scene, but in Tatum's case, the proposition seemed justified: she was obviously a 'natural' on the screen rather than just a studio-manufactured product. She stole scene after scene from her dad, not deliberately (*she* thought he was the greatest), but because she had that spontaneity and sparkle that turns all really good screen children into scene-stealers.

Tatum O'Neal was a snub-faced, extremely expressive little comic actress, a tomboy charmer with a cunning grin. Although, in *Paper Moon*, she wouldn't stand for any adult female rivals, there was no hint of illicit sex with her male crony, or even its potential development. Tatum was no 'Shirley Temple with a leer', as Tuesday Weld had been described, though her heart obviously belonged 100 per cent to her adult male companion, as Shirley's had in similar tales. But instead of the innocent thirties, this was the seventies, the 'me-decade', and what updated the child character radically was the way she cursed, smoked, drank and

swindled her way through the film. Unthinkable in earlier years even with roguish characters like Jane Withers, much of *Paper Moon's* humour lay in the contrast between Tatum's extreme youth and innocent appearance, and the gleeful way she practised all the adult vices – except for sex.

Tatum got paid $16,000 for playing in *Paper Moon* and Paramount grossed over 45 million dollars from the film, in large part because so many people found the child heroine funny and irresistible. Money talks, even louder in Hollywood than elsewhere, and new Shirley Temples do not grow on trees: it had taken 40 years to find another one. By her next film, Tatum was the highest-paid child in movie history, as well as the world's youngest Academy Award winner, as Best Supporting Actress of 1973. But here, all resemblance to Shirley Temple came to a brutal end: Shirley's first success had confirmed itself and her popularity had increased in film after film over half a dozen years, showering her studio with gold at the

rate of two or three films a year. But for Tatum the magic of *Paper Moon* never really worked again. The size of her fee was a record for a child actress for her role as the girl basketball pitcher in *The Bad News Bears* (1976) but that was really Walter Matthau's film, and she appeared again in one of Bogdanovich's unsuccessful pastiches, *Nickelodeon* (1977). In 1978 they tried to make her step into Elizabeth Taylor's horseshoes in an updated sequel to *National Velvet* called *International Velvet*, featuring her as a champion teenage showjumper. When the films in which she played a straightforward kiddy failed to keep her fans happy, they tried introducing her to the world of precocious sex, and at twelve she was offered the part of *Pretty Baby*, but her father turned it down for her. She was sexy but a virgin in *Little Darlings* (1980), but that didn't work with the public either. Then, at sixteen, she played Richard Burton's very own Lolita (*he* was going on 60), in *Circle of Two* (1980) but nobody got very excited, even though the film included Tatum's first nude scene.

By this time, it was perfectly clear to all that the *Paper Moon* miracle was not repeating itself; if Tatum had started at five, she might have had a Shirley Temple-style career. But she had started at nine and, though she was pretty enough in her teens, she lacked that element of magic – an unripe sexiness, or its tantalizing potential, that true Hollywood Lolitas must have when they reach puberty and beyond.

Tatum turned out to be a one-film star as some writers are one-novel novelists; but she certainly felt and acted like a star throughout her nymphet years. That she formed during all that time a genuine couple with a grown man – her handsome father – gave her public image a piquancy it would have lacked if she had formed the classic but duller ambitious mother-daughter duo. Tatum had spent her earliest years with her actress mother, Joanna Moore, with whom she never got along (in her teens, the rift grew so wide that she actually spat in her mother's face during a violent row). After one of those rows, at age eight she packed her suitcase and arrived at her father's house, announcing: 'I'm gonna stay.' And she did. They were very much in the public eye after the vast success of *Paper Moon*, and people goggled to see Ryan O'Neal escorting his little pre-teenager to parties, discos and nightclubs, already wearing glitter eye make-up, jewels and low-cut evening dresses. At twelve, every inch the prima donna, she fired three chauffeurs on the set of *The Bad News Bears*. At thirteen, she was running up large credit accounts at expensive Beverly Hills boutiques; she was also smoking in earnest and announcing to the world that she planned to have an affair as soon as she got the chance.

Yet, deep down, her heart still belonged to daddy. Fiercely jealous of his many girl-friends, she tagged along every time Ryan had a date and tried to pick quarrels with the ladies. Somewhere under the pseudo-sophistication, a little lost child lived in terror of losing the one and only human being who really mattered. There are touch-

ing photographs of her, already a bit large and lumpy, snuggling like a baby in her father's arms, and she found touching words to express her twelve-year-old passion for him: 'My relationship with my dad is extremely precious. Nobody in the world has a relationship like that. Me and my dad – it has nothing to do with sex. It's not perverse. Some people think like that because we're too close. People are weird.' That a twelve-year-old – even one who wore glitter make-up and danced in discos – had to insist on the fact that her relationship with her father was not perverse just because it was close says a lot about the way Hollywood Lolita's status had evolved by the seventies.

At fifteen, Tatum already seemed jaded by her life. 'You can't be friends with people who are not in the business,' she told one journalist at the time, 'they are basically jealous.' She professed to find the normal pleasures of the average teenage LA rich-kid – drugs and surfing – to be time-wasters. Five years later, while facing up to the

Left: *Roman Polanski and Nastassia Kinski. The eight years spent under the volcano of her parents' passionate and tormented marriage, left Nastassia hungry for the obsessive, all-powerful love of an older man.* Right: *With Christopher Lee in*

inevitable task of carving out an adult career for herself, Tatum found herself a different sort of notoriety among the gossip columns by falling in with another moody child star of a different sort – John McEnroe. Tennis's 'superbrat' and biggest mouth teamed up with Tatum in New York in 1983 at the height of his career, and his game appeared to deteriorate in direct proportion to the intensity and seriousness of his relationship with Tatum. But it seems that, like his arch-opponent, Bjorn Borg, McEnroe preferred not to sacrifice his new love for the pressures and million dollar rewards of the tennis circuits. (It helped of course that he was already a multi-millionaire.)

It seems appropriate that these two huge but youthful talents who spent their most successful years bad-mouthing almost everything in sight should have found mutual stability in each other's company. Now married, and with two children, it is McEnroe who has been making the tentative comeback, while Tatum, erstwhile nymphet, stays home minding the babies.

'You would be surprised by the power a girl of thirteen or fourteen can have over a man.' No Nabokov, no middle-aged Humbert Humbert made that obvious yet provocative statement, but one nymphet-extraordinary, Nastassia Kinski, rushing to the defence of her 46-year-old ex-lover, Roman Polanski, after he fled the United States to avoid facing a charge that he had raped a thirteen-year-old girl. With Nastassia – Nasti to her friends – 'nymphetolotry' took one more step out of the closet. Here was the nymphet herself coolly speaking up not for a fellow-victim but for the older man who had (theoretically at least) abducted and seduced her too when she was barely fifteen. She claimed Polanski had been victimized and unfairly condemned because he was famous. She vaunted the privilege of having been his baby mistress in these terms: 'People had warned me about him and young girls, but he was always so nice to me... He was so wonderful, so loving, so giving. He introduced me to so many things. And, yes, I fell in love with him. He took me to countries, gave me books, introduced me to the theatre. He was kind.'

Humbert Humbert too had tried to cultivate his Lolita, to travel with her, to give her books... But Lolita wanted none of it: 'To the wonderland I had to offer, my fool preferred the corniest movies, the most cloying fudge. To think that between a Hamburger and a Humberger she would – invariably, with icy precision – plump for the former.' Nastassia, on the other hand, was the dream nymphet of every Humbert: eager, compliant, loyal, grateful, and even *in love* with her Humberts (Polanski was not the only one: it is rumoured that she had already had a fling with Marcello Mastroianni, and had left Roman for the even older Milos Forman). 'I like them because they have lived,' she explained, 'and I like them to teach me things.' The ideal nymphet with her sexy angel's face and her gratitude to men over 40 for taking care of her; in his wildest dreams, Humbert could not have imagined a more perfect love object.

Yet at the same time she was a devil's daughter, sent by Old Nick to drive men mad, to lure them from the straight and narrow path, to neutralize their guilt feelings and make it seem right and proper that under-age girls should team up with libidinous lechers past their prime, in search of fresh young blood and fresh young lives to feed upon. It was appropriate that Nastassia's first major movie role was that of the devil's offspring in *To the Devil ... a Daughter* (1976), a tale of Satanism and black magic, about a young girl who becomes involved in a tug-of-war between the forces of good and evil (these were the years of *Rosemary's Baby* and *The Exorcist*). The movie was so scary that Nastassia admitted at the time: 'When I see the film, I'll probably cover my eyes.' The film was X-rated, so officially she was too young to see it then, just as Sue Lyon was not allowed to see *Lolita*.

The devil's daughter had to look angelic, like a virginal school girl; otherwise people would get suspicious and the black magic might not work. Nastassia's angel-devil duality has remained with her: one of her most

effective performances was in *Cat People* (1982), where she looked so sweet most of the time, but then turned into a ferocious, man-eating panther when you least expected it (usually during the act of love).

It was an old family tradition. Nastassia's flesh-and-blood father, Klaus Kinski, is one of the most daemonic-looking actors alive, never so powerfully as when he played Nosferatu in *Vampyr* (1978). His looks have condemned him to the role of fiends, or lunatics, or both. His personality has done the rest: he *is* Aguirre and Fitzcarraldo, fierce, obsessed, unscrupulous. 'To know Nastassia,' a close friend of the family once explained, 'you must know her parents. Brigitte is a poet, Klaus is possessed.' The little daughter grew up between the poet and the possessed, and the mass of contradictions that make up her personality simultaneously reflect the personalities of both parents.

Nastassia's parents were bohemian and nomadic. For the first eight years of her life, they dragged her about with them from hotel room to hotel room, in country after country. She was witness and participant in their erratic, passion-laden existence. The recollection of those first years was so vivid that Nastassia has memories going back to the age of two, but her impressions are incoherent: 'It was all so intense; we were reacting immediately to everything. It was the most blissful time. It was difficult, almost too right. There was such tension; we screamed and yelled and went our own ways and forgot the fight till the next one. But the family is truly my biggest love affair ever.'

All of Nastassia's duality is there: bliss and horror, screams and love, so intense, but 'almost too right'. Most of her later interviews will be expressed in this jumbled manner, angel and devil struggling to have the last word. Child of a poet and a possessed, Nastassia had inherited the poetic looks and some of the possessed personality.

When she was nine, her parents split up and divorced: Catastrophe or salvation? Both and neither. Trauma certainly. A few years later Nastassia spoke of her 'passion' for her father and yet refused to see him when he lived a few streets away from her in Beverly Hills. But the terrible shock of losing an adored tyrant of a father, who subsequently neglected his relationship with her, created the conditions propitious to the development of the future movie nymphet: a beautiful girl-child on the eve of puberty alone with a none-too-rich mother, who had long ago given up a career as a model and aspiring film actress (what else) to care for husband and child. It was not very long before Nastassia was posing nude for magazines ('I did a few things for money,' she later admitted). She left school at thirteen, 'to become a model', and became something of a streetwise kid: 'I wanted to be a woman. I was like a wild animal. I spent nights without sleeping, going to parties. My mother didn't try to contain me, she knew I had to be free.'

This is a totally normal course for a nymphet to take when she is left to run wild and discovers 'the power a girl of thirteen or fourteen can have on a man'. But many will wonder at Brigitte Kinski's *laissez-faire* attitude towards her child, letting her leave school, pose in the nude and go to all-night parties at thirteen. Was she crazy, indifferent or in league with the devil? Of course she was none of these – Brigitte was a freethinker who believed in allowing her child's good sense to protect her, although she has admitted to worrying about Nastassia's whereabouts at this time. The truth of the matter is, that short of locking her in her bedroom, Brigitte Kinski probably had little control over her extremely self-willed yet dreamy daughter's movements. But even the child, ostracized by her lifestyle, felt that something was wrong. 'Once I stopped school and started work ... people began treating me as if I was a bad person. For no reason my friends dropped me,' she sadly recalled a few years later. Her mother, however, seemed to take it all in her stride, and did not try to prevent her barely fifteen-year-old daughter from being whisked away to the far end of the world (the Seychelles) by one of her own contemporaries, the film director Roman Polanski.

Polanski was, like Humbert Humbert and Lolita, both mentor and nemesis for Nastassia Kinski. Two years after the affair ended, when she was still only seventeen and Polanski was still persona non grata in America, he cast her in the title role of *Tess*, Thomas Hardy's timeless heroine who sacrifices her sexuality to an older and socially more powerful man. This was probably Kinski's best role to date, which Polanski shrewdly suggests is because 'she wasn't required to be anything but herself'; he after all should know. Certainly, when interviewed about the role at the time the film came out, the demarcation line blurs between her own and Tess's persona. She told Clancy Sigal of *The Guardian*: 'Tess never quite says no to her rapist not because she thinks she'll like it but because ... sometimes when you're in a new situation you're so flabbergasted you don't know how to react. It's only afterwards you realize what's happened.' Can this be how she felt when she was whisked away to the Seychelles and

dressed up as a pirate to be photographed for *Vogue* by a notorious film-director more than twice her age?

Nastassia's movie presence has brought heavyweight interpretations of her character from literati like Norman Mailer, who (inevitably) compared her to Marilyn Monroe in front of the camera. Part of her resents this sort of pontificating as gross intrusion. 'I'm tired of filming, tired of everyone tearing into me, wanting a slice of me – every second of my life accounted for. I just want a private life.' If comparisons have to be made, this sounds less like Marilyn Monroe than Greta Garbo, who also made the mistake of thinking that she could keep her private life to herself.

Nastassia Kinski's life has always been lived in the public eye, and she soon became the famous daughter of a famous father. Yet by her own admission she was easily influenced by those in power – which means those she admires; the male film directors and photographers who have persuaded her to do things on and off camera

which she has sometimes regretted. Like the *Playboy* series of nude photos published in 1983. After the event she claimed embarrassment. 'It is difficult when the people you work with see these things,' she said, adding somewhat superfluously, 'it makes you feel undressed in front of them.' And she anxiously took all of the blame on herself. 'I don't blame anybody for it . . . I'm very easily trapped.' But the contradictions abound. In another interview she claimed that she was considered arrogant because she tried to protect herself: 'I sit in a box in the middle of another box called Hollywood. I may undress on the screen. Nudity in the flesh doesn't bother me. But having my mind uncovered. That scares the hell out of me.'

Nastassia finds a modicum of peace with her own mother, who discovered that many a daughter turned loose too soon in a hard world of men and money always remains Mummy's little girl. Long after Nastassia had become a star and a millionairess, with two flats in New York and two more in Paris, a journalist would write: 'Her only real home

as the sultry heroine – and victim – of the film. Right: *Sexy and innocent – two adjectives that describe Miss Kinski even better naked than when fully clothed.*

Left: *Behind Nastassia Kinski's glamorous
façade the signs of exhaustion are already
apparent: 'I'm so tired ... I've lived so
much.'* Right: *Good friends on and off the*

and resting place is her mother's flat in Munich. Brigitte is still Nastassia's only close friend and confidante – they often fight, but quickly patch up the quarrels.' A little shell-shocked from life, she feels most secure where she can be and act the child, she who was treated as a woman when she was still a child. Mother's flat is the one place where sex will not rear its ugly head. 'I'm so tired... I've lived so much,' the moody, tear-prone Nastassia constantly repeated in interviews given when she was only just out of her teens. More recently, friendships such as the one she struck up with Jodie Foster, a girl with the same Hollywood experiences to an extent, have helped her, in spite of Nastassia's rather aggressive femininity which claimed that women 'are not my best friends'. Craving love, she has thrown herself wholeheartedly into motherhood, the one sure way of receiving unlimited and unquestioning devotion.

This Lolita is still looking for the *real* father she has lost; lovers and husbands are never completely satisfactory in that role,

however vast the age-gap. 'The love I felt for him was in many ways like a family love,' she revealingly said of Polanski, 'but as a director he was ten times more wonderful than as a lover.' She had refused to marry him, but the much older man she did marry, Arab businessman Ibrahim Moussa fared little better: soon after they were married Nastassia walked out on him while she was expecting their second child, and since then their volatile relationship has seen many rows and reconciliations. He too had to admit: 'I was more of a father to her than a husband.'

To the Devil, a Daughter, to drive men mad at will. Nastassia was the dream nymphet who has turned dream child-woman. She has even inherited much of her father's acting talent, has been praised to the skies for her role in *Tess*, in *Cat People* (1982), in *Maria's Lovers* (1984) and in *Paris, Texas* (1984); she has worked with such distinguished directors as Wim Wenders, Alberto Lattuada, Francis Coppola, Paul Schrader, Tony Richardson and Andrei Konchalovsky. Yet like another devil's daughter, Arletty, in *Les Visiteurs du Soir*, there is a weary, far-away expression in her eyes: driving men mad is a dull affair, especially when you've done it so effortlessly since you were thirteen. What might make a real change, introduce a note of excitement, perhaps even be truly fulfilling, would be to know the fate to which most women are condemned from the start. Which is why the brooding, almond-shaped eyes of the devil's daughter actually gleam a little when she says: 'I would like to live in a big house with animals and a family, with everybody doing their own thing. I want to grow old and become a grandmother.'

Any discussion of Nastassia Kinski's career always seems overshadowed by the brooding if diminutive presence of the Polish director, Roman Polanski. Eyebrows were raised but no-one in the decadent European intellectual world he inhabited seemed particularly shocked by his liaison with Klaus Kinski's teenage daughter – even with a thirty-year age difference. It was a different matter in the United States however when his predilection for underage sex

set of Hotel New Hampshire, *Nastassia and Jodie Foster's colourful Hollywood experiences are a common bond.*

finally overstepped the mark. On March 11th, 1977, fifty years after the Chaplin-Lilita McMurray scandal, thirty-five years after the first Errol Flynn nymphet trial, Polanski was arrested on charges of child-molesting. Like Chaplin, Polanski discovered that Hollywood's judgment can still be puritanical and stern under the sophisticated, anything-goes façade. Like Nabokov's Humbert Humbert, both men were Europeans which made them, by definition, corrupt in the eyes of a large section of American public opinion. Both the girls involved were American and extremely young, thus almost by definition wholesome and innocent. The role played by the mothers in both cases was ambivalent, to say the least: were they instigators, accomplices, or genuinely ignorant of the danger their little girls ran in the company of such men?

Both Chaplin and Polanski had long since made their sexual preference for immature girls more or less public, Chaplin by his earlier affair with fifteen-year-old Mildred Harris, Polanski in his life-style and declarations to the press. Pursued relentlessly by cameramen at the 1977 Cannes Film Festival while walking arm in arm with Nastassia, Polanski lost his cool and turned on them, screaming 'I've never hidden the fact that I love young girls . Once and for all, I love very young girls'. In fact this episode put paid to his relationship with Nastassia, although she remained startlingly loyal to him. One of his former bedmates had said in print: 'When I see him coming on to some young girl, I want to say to her she should give this guy a wide berth.' Another was even more explicit, stating that men like Polanski have 'spent their lifetime in sexual over-indulgence, so they can no longer relate sexually to ordinary women... They are obsessed with virgins. And where are you most likely to find these? Among little girls, of course.' Thus it is difficult to believe that the mothers of Lilita McMurray and Polanski's 'Sandra' did not know what was going on, given the fact that both lived in Los Angeles and were connected with the movies.

is the pseudonym used by Polanski in his autobiography.)

After spending six weeks in prison after his arrest, Polanski chose to flee before the trial, and he still faces prosecution in the US. At the time it happened, Polanski was looking for adolescent girls to photograph for *Vogue*. 'I proposed to show girls as they really were these days – sexy, pert, thoroughly human,' he said. Sandra, a juvenile TV commercial model, had been described to him as a 'fabulous-looking teenager', but when he met her he found 'nothing sensational' about her.

Did her mother, Jane, think, as Nastassia Kinski's mother thought, that Polanski was 'like some God sent from Heaven to help her'? A small-time actress herself, she must have construed the offer as a miraculous piece of luck for her 'baby', and willingly let her go off alone with the notorious 'chickenhawk' for some semi-nude photographic sessions on a deserted hillside. These sessions culminated some days later in Jack Nicholson's empty house, with champagne, a then fashionable drug called Quaalude, and sex on a sofa.

Polanski speaks of 'Sandra's experience and lack of inhibition', though he admits she didn't seem to enjoy the experience much. He had asked her how old she was when she first had sex, and was 'shaken' when she told him she had started at eight with 'a kid down the street', adding, 'at that age you don't even know what's going on.' The very fact that Polanski was asking Sandra questions as intimate as these almost precludes the possibility that he had not also asked her what age she was at the time of the affair. And Polanski was not so naïve as to think there was no difference between the inexpert fumblings of pre-pubescent kids of the same age and full sexual intercourse with a middle-aged man of 44. Polanski's claim that he thought Sandra was eighteen is belied by his own recollections of their conversations, which were obviously attuned to someone very much younger.

Like many middle-aged paedophiles Polanski found it difficult to face the reality of the charges which were brought against

The fact that the mother may be accomplice – even instigator – does not exonerate the man involved, any more than the little girl's seductiveness and eventual consent turns her into the seducer. At twelve or thirteen, she remains the victim and the man the criminal: Nabokov insisted on this fact throughout *Lolita*, which was a highly moralistic novel in that respect. Nor does Polanski's allegation that he did not know the girl's real age – thirteen – make him any the less to blame; he could – and probably did – ask. In his autobiography, *Roman*, Polanski makes exactly the same excuse for bedding fifteen-year-old Nastassia Kinksi on the first night he met her. Unlike Errol Flynn, who got off the hook from one of his statutory rape charges by claiming the girl lied about her age, at least Polanski is honest enough to refuse to put the blame on his young girlfriends in that way. Instead he merely claims that he didn't bother to enquire, and thought they were much older.

Like most autobiographies, Polanski's appears straightforward, but also contains a lot of self-justification in his description of the 'Sandra' case that wrecked his thriving Hollywood career. (As the girl was a minor, her real name was never revealed. 'Sandra'

him: 'I couldn't equate what had happened the day before with rape in any form,' he wrote. 'Nothing in my life had prepared me for the idea that I might be a criminal.' A little champagne after a jacuzzi session, a little pill-popping and a little sex with a pretty and apparently not too reluctant girl... For Polanski, what could be more agreeably Californian and relaxing – just like a million other little flings. But this time, the girl's mother blew the whistle on him. The Grand Jury charges brought against him after she complained to the police were bleak indeed: 'Furnishing a controlled substance to a minor; committing a lewd or lascivious act; having unlawful sexual intercourse; perversion; sodomy; and rape by use of drugs.' These charges recognized that however receptive the thirteen-year-old Sandra may have appeared, there is no doubt that Polanski was breaking the law. Sex with a minor in California – as in most US States and countries outside the US – is deemed statutory rape. Polanski may have thought he hadn't coerced her, but he did use champagne, quaaludes and the power of his position in the movie world to get what he wanted. He didn't need to use *physical* force.

Polanski is a born survivor: he survived the Krakow ghetto and the Jewish holocaust; he survived the East-West transition when he moved from his native Poland to France; he survived the appalling murder of his wife, Sharon Tate, at the hands of the Charles Manson sect; he has now survived the charges of rape and the stay in jail which turned him into an outlaw and a runaway once more. Many another man's career and spirit would have been broken by the Sandra ordeal: not Polanski's. A year later his reputation as film director and artist soared to new heights with the shooting of *Tess* (1978), the film that also launched his protegee, Nastassia Kinski. 'I am widely regarded, I know, as an evil, profligate dwarf. My friends – and the women in my life – know otherwise. Many women seem irresistibly attracted by notoriety, and many – especially since the Los Angeles affair – are eager to meet me,' he smugly concludes in

his autobiography. Those who find the moral of the story hard to swallow can take some comfort in the fact that, by his own admission, Polanski is not a happy man. As he puts it: 'I know in my heart of hearts that the spirit of laughter has deserted me. It isn't just that success has left me jaded or that I've been soured by tragedy and my own follies. I seem to be toiling to no discernible purpose. I feel I've lost the right to innocence, to a pure appreciation of life's pleasure.'

More than ten years have passed since Polanski fled from America, and now he lives his life in a style perhaps better suited to his years. 'I am at the age I don't like to be reminded of', he said just after his fiftieth birthday. 'Since 30 I stopped enjoying my birthdays although strangely enough I have always felt 30 years old ever since.' Perhaps this makes one of his most recent liaisons – with a statuesque Frenchwoman in her forties with (significantly) two strapping teenage sons – feel like an affair with an older woman. 'I have a great relationship with very young women or women of a certain age,' he said recently. 'I do not have a good relationship with women in their thirties.' Somewhat ingenuously, he added, 'What I like about younger women is that they don't use sex appeal to further their social positions or career.' (In Hollywood, they don't need to – their mothers do it for them.)

Now, after working in the theatre in his native Poland and directing films in Europe, Polanski is thinking about mending fences in Hollywood by turning himself in to 'clear his name'. Friends in California think that the District Attorney's office might look more favourably on his case after so much time. But even so, it is doubtful whether Polanski can ever shake off his reputation as a Hollywood Humbert – the *paparazzi* have caught him in the company of teenagers much too frequently for the international tabloids to let him alone. And even though his most famous Lolita, Nastassia Kinski, has insisted that it 'wasn't a crime, just a private thing between two people', the indictment and conviction remain on record.

JODIE FOSTER
The knowing look of the all-American girl-child gave her nymphet appeal whether as a Disney heroine or a twelve-year-old hooker

BROOKE SHIELDS
A pretty baby saddled with being 'the most beautiful woman in the world' at the age of eleven

8. Miss Coppertone versus Miss Ivory Snow

Once upon a time, there were two baby girls. One had blond hair, the other dark. Both had blue eyes that stared not-so-innocently upon the wide wide world: it is difficult to remain innocent for long when problems of auditions, money, work and haggling over contracts beset one at an age when other tots are riding tricycles around suburban backyards, when there is no daddy at home, only a mommy struggling with her own emotional problems of divorce, loneliness, depression and alcoholism, when *you* are the crutch, the salvation, the bread-winner, your mommy's mommy, in a way, though you may be only three years old. For like so many Hollywood Lolitas before them, both baby girls had too little daddy and too much mommy in their early lives. The parents of blonde baby Jodie Foster divorced five months after she was born. The parents of brunette baby Brooke Shields got married five months after she was conceived and divorced a few months after her birth. The fathers were thus nebulous figures in the early lives of their daughters. 'I don't discuss my father because he has nothing to do with my life. I've seen him a couple of times but he hasn't been in touch with me,' a growing-up Jodie later explained when asked about her father, who was in the Los Angeles real estate business. 'I'm no stage father,' Brooke's dad said dismissively of his daughter's career, after her most notorious film role, in *Pretty Baby*, had hit the headlines. It seems he disapproved of the whole business, but not enough to interfere, for by then he had a busy career of his own as a New York perfume executive, another wife and four more children to worry about.

If the fathers were only vague, remote figures in the lives of their little girls, the mothers more than made up for that ab-sence by being overwhelmingly, stiflingly present, living off, by, through and for their tiny daughters, relentlessly peddling and protecting them, sheltering their babies even as they exploited (and – some said – sexploited) the children's youthful charms. Brooke Shields and Jodie Foster, though rivals to the death on the Hollywood Lolita market, are said to be pals. Do Terri Shields and Brandy Foster know and like – or at least respect – each other? By all accounts, they are sisters under the skin: ambitious, shrewd, calculating businesswomen, outwardly strong but probably vulnerable and mixed-up underneath. Nabokov, the expert on nymphets and their mothers, had this to say of *his* Lolita's mama, Charlotte Haze: 'Charlotte rapped with her ring finger and sauntered in. How different were her movements from those of my Lolita, when she used to visit me in her dear dirty blue jeans, smelling of orchards in nymphetland; awkward and fey, and dimly depraved, the lower buttons of her shirt unfastened. Let me tell you, however, something. Behind the brashness of little Haze, and the poise of big Haze, a trickle of shy life ran that tasted the same, that murmured the same.' Doubtless, Nabokov would have instantly diagnosed those mysterious resemblances that surely existed between the fiery, aggressive Terri and the cool, retiring Brooke, between the forceful, pushy Brandy and the detached, elusive Jodie.

The two baby girls presumably started off like all other babies: in a whirl of feeding bottles, diapers, angry squalls and contented gurgles. But their carefree babyhood days were brief. The one called Brookie, legend has it, was being wheeled in her pram one day when a mysterious, aging film-star who had retired from the screen many years earlier, peered at the infant through the

luxuriant nut-brown hair, was still bald as an egg, and only ten months old, when she started her career, selling soap. As 'Miss Ivory Snow', Brookie was the cleanest, if not yet the prettiest, baby in the world. Jodie did not get involved in the hazardous business of selling her little body for a living until she was all of three years old, when she became 'Miss Coppertone', the kiddie who bared her bottom to the world to sell suntan lotion.

Like so many Hollywood Lolita mothers, Terri Shields had had messianic expectations for her daughter long before then: 'Brooke is a miracle,' she was to declare. 'When she was only five days old I knew that she was the most beautiful thing I'd ever seen in my life and that her beauty was going to contribute to mankind.' To another interviewer, she put it less rhapsodically: 'I knew she was going to be a millionaire the first day I brought her home from the hospital.' Apparently, she never doubted that she possessed in her child a piece of highly saleable merchandize. When she

dark glasses behind which she always hid, exclaiming in her inimitable Swedish accent: 'That child is magnificent! She will go far!' Legend or proud mother's justification of predestination? The two are often indistinguishable when Hollywood Lolita's mother sets out to create her daughter's myth.

No aging star gasped at the beauty of the little blonde baby, however, and none probably ever will. She was not beautiful, not even Shirley Temple cute, but she had what Americans liked in latter-day nymphets such as Sue Lyon and Tuesday Weld: that fair, wholesome, kid-next-door look, rendered ambivalent by eyes that were too knowing, a wry, off-hand expression that hinted an experience well beyond one's real age, and a husky, ironic tone of voice that speaks with the wisdom of the streets. Even her name was banal and girl-next-doorish: no glamorous, exotic or foreign-sounding consonants, no Rita, no Ava, no Raquel or Greta, just plain, all-American Jodie Foster.

The other baby girl, the one with the

and her ambitious mother. Right: *The knowing Brooke Shields, aged twelve. 'Sure I knew what was going on with the sex scenes and everything in New Orleans. I just didn't say so.'*

took her baby for the first audition, she described how 'there were about 400 mothers there, and some of them had come from as far as Detroit and Michigan. I felt so sorry for them, because when I walked in with Brookie they hadn't got a chance.'

Jodie Foster's first break into the world of fame, fortune and high finance came about quite differently. Back in those days, her eight-year-old brother Buddy was the family breadwinner, earning $25,000 a year from commercials. It was he who went to the Coppertone suncream audition with mother Brandy. Baby Jodie tagged along because, as Brandy explained, 'I couldn't leave her in the car, so she had to come with us'. She did. And she got the job.

The subsequent careers of the two little girls were oddly parallel, so much so that to describe each one in turn becomes tediously repetitive. The elder one, blonde Jodie (born in 1962), continued to make commercials, and kept her family in the style to which it became accustomed. But she also moved over into acting, in TV series and

films, and was a well-known child actress by the time she was ten, with leading roles in Disney Studio movies for kids, and various parts playing people's kid sister or daughter. (Her cameo role as the streetwise nine-year-old who knows how to shoplift, in *Alice Doesn't Live Here Anymore* (1974) is one of the high points of a very good film.)

Brooke Shields' pre-pubescent acting career was less distinguished, though, like Elizabeth Taylor, she grew to be a ravishing child, and her famous nut-brown hair had grown so long that she could sit on it by the time she was four. In fact, she was almost too pretty to model, the agents told her mother. Too pretty to impersonate the average American kid who is the darling of commercials. Yet her perfection could sell products that claimed perfection would result from regular use: Ivory Snow soap would give you a flawless complexion – like Brooke's; Breck shampoo would give you glorious hair – like Brooke's; Colgate toothpaste would make your teeth dazzling white – like Brooke's. Her film career was yet to

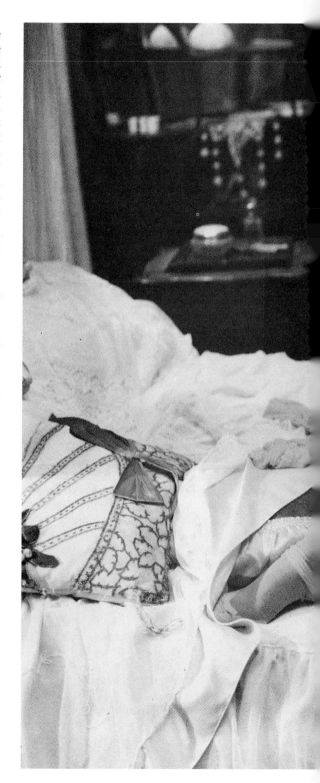

Brooke at her most coquettish in Pretty Baby. *The world's sexiest eleven-year-old is now twelve, but she's showing no signs of losing her charm.*

come: it is not easy to find roles for little girls who have excessive beauty with little acting talent to match. Brookie was stabbed to death by a religious maniac in *Alice, Sweet Alice* (*Communion* in Britain, 1977) when she was nine. A small role she played in Woody Allen's *Annie Hall* (1978) was cut during editing. But mother Terri did not wait until her daughter was eleven and offered the child prostitute part in *Pretty Baby* (1978) to grasp her daughter's sexual potential. Some mothers may be satisfied with a squeaky clean Colgate image and more money than they could hope to spend, but others may want to see their child's sexuality exposed even before they have reached sexual maturity.

Listen to Terri describing the first time her daughter was asked to pose nude for something a bit more suggestive than soap: 'When Brooke was eight, she was asked to pose nude, and it was no problem. She just took her clothes off, put her foot on a chair. "This is the sort of thing you want?"' Where-upon the proud Terri jumps up and cheer-fully assumes a typical porno pose to show what she means. Presumably, it was those steamy shots which, a few years later, Mrs Shields tried so hard to stop from going on public display on the grounds that they could ruin her daughter's image. The judge agreed the pictures were so lascivious that 'the sale of large volumes of the photo-graphs would result in serious injury to Miss Shields'. Yet the Shields' lost the battle in the end, for as the photographer's lawyer sneer-ingly argued, Brooke Shields was 'no Shirley Temple... She is portrayed as a young vamp and a harlot, the Lolita of her generation'.

The fourteen-year-old Brooke was to relate another revealing anecdote: 'One day, my mother had a guest in our New York apartment. I must have been about ten. On the piano, there was a photograph of me in a rather sexy outfit and the gentleman in question was in ecstasies over the picture: "What a pity you didn't invite that girl this evening. She looks so great." My mother replied: "I didn't invite her, but she's here. It's my daugher. She's ten years old and she's asleep in the next room."' Mrs Shields

was much amused by her guest's embarrassment and seemed to revel in her precocious daughter's ability to arouse a lust in men she had no intention of letting them assuage.

Terri's enjoyment of her child's sex appeal was not necessarily shared by little Brooke. 'So men are turned on by Brooke,' Terri once gloated to an interviewer, 'that's their problem. Brooke has always had that sensual look... Even Elizabeth Taylor didn't have it at her age.' At this point in the interview, Brooke chipped in: 'I don't try to look sexy, really I don't. It's just the way I am'. 'You see! She's really just a normal kid,' her mother responded, delighted to have her cake and to eat it too; but the next moment she was afraid she might be taken too literally and added hastily: 'Of course, she is a bombshell. She prefers older men, but at the moment she's going through puberty and is not sure whether to suck her thumb or go out on a date.' All this maternal revelling in a daughter's erotic powers, in that young lady's presence, would seem somewhat distasteful even if the girl were

grown up. But it is hard to know how to describe it when one realizes that Brooke was eleven years old at the time. But then she was already being touted as the World's Sexiest Eleven-Year-Old, and this was actually before *Pretty Baby* was released. A few months after the release of the film, she was asked if the nude scenes in *Pretty Baby* bothered her. 'Not when we were shooting them,' she said 'but I was younger then. You don't bother with taking off your clothes when you're only eleven. But maybe I wouldn't do it now that I'm older.' Brooke was all of twelve years old at the time.

Three years before *Pretty Baby*, the blonde baby girl, Jodie Foster, had already created a sensation at the ripe old age of twelve, playing a child prostitute in Martin Scorsese's *Taxi Driver* (1976). How does one skip from Walt Disney movies and playing Becky in *Tom Sawyer* to such a role within a year or so? Little Brooke Shields confessed after making *Pretty Baby* that she would rather have been in a Walt Disney movie. But Jodie was blasé after playing so many juvenile roles in films for juveniles. Nor were all her memories of those days carefree; she still shuddered at the recollection of falling into a toilet at the age of four during one film, and being bitten by a lion on her famous backside when she was nine. She professed to despise the classic child-star type and spoke scornfully of her predecessors. 'I hate the idea that everybody thinks if a kid's going to be an actress it means that she has to play Shirley Temple or someone's little sister,' she once declared, adding on another occasion: 'In the days of those dumb juveniles like Margaret O'Brien and Elizabeth Taylor, all they were asked to do was look cute and say they loved Daddy and hug Lassie.'

This was probably an *a posteriori* justification of the highly controversial decision to make a twelve-year-old play the role of a fully-fledged hooker, complete with hot pants, a shady pimp and a cynical c'mon. Of course, the decision was not hers but her mother's. She had already worked with Scorsese on *Alice Doesn't Live Here Any More*, but even so, when Scorsese sent them

the script, Jodie was to recall: 'I thought this was a great part for a 21-year-old. I couldn't believe they were offering it to me... At first I didn't want to do it.' Nor could the California welfare authorities believe that Mrs Foster would allow her child to play in so grim a saga of death and depravity. But mother always knows best, or at least thinks she does. 'I was determined to win,' said Brandy. 'Here was some board trying to tell me what was too adult for my own daughter. When they turned us down, I decided right, we would beat them... As a mother, Jodie's morals are my concern.' Jodie's brother, Buddy, also felt that the child's morals were his concern and objected violently to the idea, but Mrs Foster battled on. Her daughter could not miss the opportunity of playing opposite Robert de Niro, and that was that.

In the end, the welfare authorities stepped down and agreed on condition Jodie underwent a four-hour session with a psychiatrist from the University of California at Los Angeles, who had to rule on her mental stability. 'I suppose they figured that if I was willing to play a part like that, I had to be insane,' Jodie laughed. The psychiatrists may not have been altogether reassured to hear how this twelve-year-old countered their objections that she might suffer psychological damage if she impersonated a whore and met real prostitutes: 'I told them that there was nothing to worry about on that score as I'd known all about it for ages. You learn quickly when you start out so young in show business!' Soon, young Jodie was wobbling on platform heels, decked out in satin mini shorts, spending a month of her school vacation doing 'research' for the part in New York's red-light district, while a happy Brandy shopped and cooked for her 'wonderful little girl'. After all, she had already starred as a hooker in the all-juvenile British gangster film parody, *Bugsy Malone* (released 1976), but people seemed to cast a blind eye over that – after all it was only kids play-acting, wasn't it. Wasn't it? That *Taxi Driver* brought Jodie world-fame proved how clever Brandy had been at

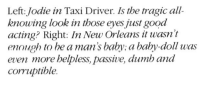

Left: *Jodie* in Taxi Driver. *Is the tragic all-knowing look in those eyes just good acting?* Right: *In New Orleans it wasn't enough to be a man's baby; a baby-doll was even more helpless, passive, dumb and corruptible.*

managing her daughter's career. As Jodie said to Andy Warhol a couple of years later: 'You always find that success comes from a strong mother influence... We're a team. We're like Laurel and Hardy.'

Three years after the furore over *Taxi Driver*, boards of welfare had more or less given up trying to save Hollywood's Lolitas from their mothers' ambitions and from directors' ambitions to create an ever greater sexual sensation in their movies. Louis Malle, the French director who had already created quite a sensation in France with *Le Souffle Au Coeur*, a film about a very young boy's sexual initiation by his own mother, was all ready to conquer Hollywood with a new soft-focus tale of how a consenting child is sexually initiated by an adult. To find something even more shocking than incest was not difficult. How about the story of a little girl who grows up in a New Orleans brothel at the turn of the century, whose

prostitute mother decides the time has come for the kid to pay her own way and auctions her off to the highest bidder after exhibiting her in the buff on a silver platter to potential purchasers? A few years earlier, a film on that topic would have been deemed too daring even if the girl had been over eighteen and had defended her virtue to the death (a bit like Leslie Caron in *Gigi*). But now, the girl was twelve and willing.

Though it aroused a great deal of opposition and was denounced as child pornography, though it was banned by several communities and cities in the States and held up in Britain for a year while the Censor considered what cuts to make and what certificate to give, if any, nevertheless *Pretty Baby* paid off. It was released and shown almost everywhere. Brooke's sex scenes were considerably more explicit than Jodie's in *Taxi Driver*, and the story of a mother selling her daughter for profit was even uglier than that of a lover-pimp doing the same to child-whore Iris, who was a runaway from a normal home. Yet *Pretty Baby* shocked less than *Taxi Driver* because the whorehouse setting, costumes and photography were soft, clean, pretty – and unreal. Everything about the earlier film had been grimly realistic and ugly. Little Jodie had seemed pathetically tainted and corrupted by the sordid world she moved in. But Brooke seemed to retain her sweet innocence and to remain uncorrupted by all the vice she had witnessed from her tenderest years. Miss Coppertone's hide was tanned by the seamy light of the sin-ridden city, while Miss Ivory Snow's complexion stayed squeaky clean throughout. At least *Taxi Driver* attempted to be honest in its depressing portrayal of a child of twelve doing what no child of twelve should be doing. Whereas *Pretty Baby* whispered mendaciously: 'Isn't it all quite natural and beautiful? This little girl *likes* having her body sold to and pawed by ugly old men like you.'

Predictably, *Pretty Baby* did for Brooke what *Taxi Driver* had done for Jodie. She became 'The World's Youngest Sex Symbol', to her mother's utter delight, though Terri's

drinking problem had got her fired from the set and arrested and gaoled for drunken driving during shooting. How much or how little had the eleven-year-old Brooke understood of the story and of her part? Her chaperone – a close friend of Terri's – insisted that 'we try to keep Brooke away from the sex scenes as much as possible. She doesn't really understand them. They're not shot in sequence, so she doesn't follow the story.' Brooke's version was quite different: 'Sure, I knew what was going on with the sex scenes and everything in New Orleans. I just didn't say so. I very often pretend I don't know what's going on. It works better for me... I'd have to be dumb not to know!'

Which is the prettier baby of the two baby girls turned Hollywood Lolita in the seventies? Miss Coppertone or Miss Ivory Snow? Blonde baby playing twelve-year-old whore Iris or brown-haired baby playing twelve-year-old whore Violet? Two pretty babies lost in an ugly world of big money and porn-hungry audiences always on the lookout for new, even sicker kicks. Pretty babies conditioned from their earliest childhood to strip on demand if the price is right. Pretty babies floundering a little as they cast about for some moral argument to the story of their lives and to the lives of the characters they played: Iris had become a whore to flee her stifling middle-class family in *Taxi Driver*. But the child who played Violet in *Pretty Baby* was to sigh: 'There was a family feeling about a brothel in those days.'

And what happens when cute little misses who have seen it all before they reach their teens grow up and become big girls? For Jodie Foster there was an unpleasant sequel to her *Taxi Driver* appearance. In 1979 John Hinckley, obsessed by Jodie in the film, attempted to assassinate newly-elected President Ronald Reagan as a way, he claimed, of proving his love for her. As a result, Jodie herself became the victim of death threats, perpetuating in real life her screen persona of victimized youth. She was accompanied by bodyguards for some time after the Hinkley incident, and chafes at the

way this macabre incident has clung to her over the years, 'Why do I have to be remembered as the Technicolor representation of some bizarre incident I had nothing to do with, some empty vessel for people to fill up with their own ideas and neuroses?' she complained bitterly in 1988.

But this is the price Jodie Foster is still having to pay for her role as nymphet whore in *Taxi Driver*, the part that the Welfare Authorities in California tried to stop her playing – with hindsight perhaps Jodie and her mother might credit them with some sense after all. For Jodie is still managed by Brandy, and apart from the Hinkley episode which she hates to be reminded of – 'It's like a scar I have to carry around with me' – seems to have come out of nymphet-land more or less in one piece. There is a toughness in Jodie Foster's opinions which isn't always reflected in her film roles, however.

'I realize that I am a role model for a lot of young women,' she once said, 'I'm not an activist but I don't take films where I play some sort of weak masochistic girl who can't wait to be beaten up by some man – unless it is to prove the point that it shouldn't happen.' This statement is now difficult to reconcile with her more recent screen appearances. She was subjected to attempted rape, a lesbian affair and incest with her screen brother in *Hotel New Hampshire*, a pet project she herself initiated with her friend Nastassia Kinski in 1985. In a later interview Jodie eulogized about the incest scene as 'a beautiful, sweet love affair', perhaps because it was played alongside 'brat pack' heart-throb Rob Lowe, but she was more circumspect in her comments on a gang rape inflicted on her in a later film, *The Accused*, 'It was one of the most cruel, devastating, overwhelming experiences I've ever gone through,' she admitted, although in the film the girl goes on to face her attackers in court and they are convicted.

It is surprising even so that she goes on accepting parts which offer the same sort of sexual victimization at the mercy of the uncontrolled, often psychotic, passions of

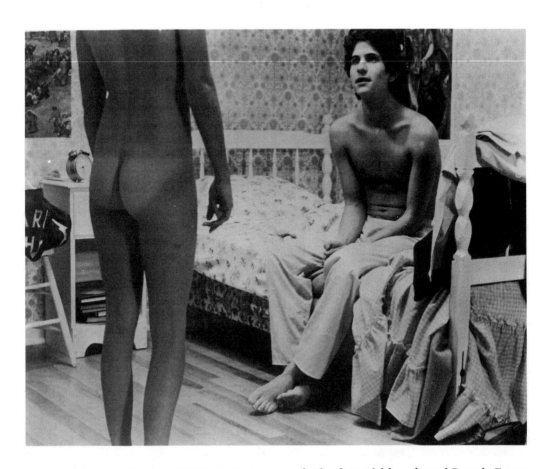

men. In *The Five Corners* (1988), Jodie as sweet, wholesome Linda is molested by Heinz, the local no-good and a former lover of hers, who batters a penguin to death as a way of expressing how he feels for her. Interestingly, Jodie explains that she can relate to Linda's maternal inclination to take care of Heinz as a way of 'supporting the underdog', even if as in this case the under-dog turns out to be a demented psychopath, who knocks her senseless in the subway and then carries her like a rag doll under his arm for most of the film. Supporting this sort of underdog sits uneasily with her reasons for taking the part in *The Accused* because it was an 'inspiring story of female strength'.

The side of Jodie which seems to seek out sexually-motivated violence on screen fits uneasily with the off-screen reality of an intelligent, perceptive, street-smart career

girl. The formidably cultured Brandy Foster groomed Jodie not only for a precocious career as a pre-pubescent movie star, but also gave her the best education money and determination could muster. A glittering academic career in Los Angeles' exclusive Lycée Français culminated quite naturally in Jodie becoming a bright student at Yale, one of America's top universities. As she put it, she worked her way through college as an English major in the way she knew best, 'in the safe bosom of my other family, a 45-person film crew'. She also made in-roads into journalism, doing interviews for Andy Warhol's *Interview* magazine, during one of which she struck up a lasting friendship with Nastassia Kinski. Jodie now expresses a keen desire to put her considerable brain power to practical use on the other side of the camera as a director – whether she will make this transition from 'empty vessel' to

line. Right: *Brooke looks far happier in the arms of a boy her own age in* Blue Lagoon *than in those of the old men who preyed on her in* Pretty Baby.

movie maestro remains to be seen.

Brooke Shields' climb into adulthood is more ambivalent. Like Jodie she showed herself to have brains, and went to Princeton to major in French literature. She struggled against loneliness at first. Her fellow students cold-shouldered her; 'I was shattered,' she recalled. 'Everyone thought I was just a movie star playing at being a student. They all thought it was cool to ignore me and I was heartbroken.' Until of course Brooke's academic results showed that she wasn't just a pretty face. And while she was at Princeton Terri Shields made sure the Brooke Shields money machine continued to pay out – with Calvin Klein jeans commercials ('Between me and my Calvins there's absolutely nothing'), a paperback advice book for teenagers called *On Your Own*, and film roles in *Sahara* and *Brenda Starr*. But Brooke never missed a class because of work and it has

meant sacrifices – one of the reasons she lost the Audrey Hepburn role in the TV movie remake of *Roman Holiday* was because it couldn't be fitted in with the completion of her studies – but she had the satisfaction of graduating with a coveted Fulbright Scholarship to study for a year outside the US in the place of her choice. At her graduation ceremony she wasn't expecting the massed ranks of the world's press and burst into tears – but at the hastily convened press conference after the ceremony (probably organized at Terri's suggestion), Brooke let down her guard for a single, revealing moment. Justifiably proud of her achievement she said of her graduation: 'I did this. I did it in four years and it was hard. I want everyone to know that.' And in all her twenty-two years, it was probably the only thing she had done without any help from her mother.

Conclusion

'You can't be anyone's little girl forever.'

Tatum O'Neal

In her memoirs, *The Movies, Mr Griffith and Me*, Lillian Gish described her first vision of Hollywood's great creator of screen 'nymphets'. She was sitting at the foot of a staircase with her sister Dorothy when D.W. Griffith came down the stairs, looking immensely tall and striking to the tiny, child-like fifteen-year-old. He was singing *Là ci darem la mano*, the song Mozart's Don Giovanni sings to Zerlina, the naïve peasant girl, when he wants to entice her into his house to seduce her: 'There we'll take hands and you will whisper "Yes". Come my dear treasure... I will change your fate!'

In this tender duet, the bargain is clear: Don Giovanni offers to make the young girl's fortune if she gives herself to him. She half-heartedly resists, admitting that she's tempted but afraid that he will cheat her, so Griffith's meaning was crystal clear. Every Hollywood Lolita's dilemma is symbolized by the fateful meeting described by Miss Gish; it can make or break her whole life. The fact that Lillian Gish's mother was present and was clearly thrilled by the great director's interest in her stunning daughter makes the encounter even more symbolic.

The bargain may be an honest one, as it was in this case: the great man asks her for her beauty, youth and acting talent in exchange for his power, status and capacity to turn her into a screen myth. Well into her nineties, Lillian Gish is still acting and still reaping the benefits of her long association with Griffith. Often, however, the bargain is no more than a false promise that leads to loss of innocence and illusions, with nothing given in return. Even when the offer is a loyal one and the girl has no hesitation in accepting it, she may live to rue the day she met the Svengali who set her on the course to stardom too young and too defenceless. Judy Garland forever cursed her studio for what it had done to her in her early teens. Sue Lyon, now a dejected-looking housewife hiding behind dark glasses, still shudders at the recollection of what playing Lolita did to her life. Brooke Shields, on the other hand, wrote her graduation thesis on the films of Louis Malle, who directed her in *Pretty Baby*. And Shirley Temple, who said she couldn't wait to be grown up when she was a little girl, now looks back with wry amusement and detachment on that period of her life.

Ambivalence is what the movie nymphet is all about: our ambivalent appreciation of her persona; the director's ambivalent presentation of her (as someone wrote of the teenage Nastassia Kinski: 'She combines the innocent look of an angel with the guilty appeal of a sex kitten'); and the young girl's own ambivalence about herself and the feelings she inspires. Feminists, wary of sexual ambivalence even in its more artistic forms, have loudly spoken out against what they themselves baptized 'the Lolita syndrome'. 'Women Against Pornography' organized a demonstration on the opening night of Edward Albee's stage adaptation of *Lolita* in New York. In an age where the sexual abuse of children has been revealed – like rape – to be far more widespread than had been previously suspected, their arguments cannot be dismissed out of hand: 'Pushed by every facet of the media – from

Calvin Klein jeans ads to art films like *Pretty Baby* – "the Lolita syndrome" promotes the sexual abuse of little girls by portraying them as sex objects and seductresses.'

There are, however, degrees in everything. Everyone hates the sexual exploitation of the young, even the exploiters themselves in many cases. But what one individual (or one age) finds distasteful, well-nigh criminal, another finds morally acceptable and natural. What is hard to know is where the line must be drawn, especially as sexual *mores* and laws change all the time. Though the age of consent and the onset of puberty decrease with the passage of time, we are still uneasy when films graphically portray young girls getting sexually involved with much older men. We wonder how it affects the girls in real life, and how healthy it is to depict such events on a screen, even when it is made clear that no-one approves of what is going on.

Albee's facile argument was that 'it is Lolita who seduces Humbert. It is the exploitation of the adult by the child'. Errol Flynn and Roman Polanski have said much the same thing in their time. England's latest screen nymphet, the toothsome Emily Lloyd, does indeed flaunt her bared legs for all Dirty Old Men to covet in *Wish You Were Here* (1987); yet at the end of the film it is she who is the victim, she who is left pushing the pram containing the wages of her 'sin' with a nasty Humbert Humbert. Who has seduced who? That is not the question. The real issue is that the weaker of two parties must always be protected against the stronger. Nabokov's Humbert Humbert knew this and fully accepted all the blame for having *allowed* himself to be seduced by Lolita. The child innocently believed that sex was just a silly game, little guessing that it would wreck her whole life. But then how can an inexperienced twelve-year-old be expected to know that?

The great Hollywood Lolitas of the twentieth century are now old ladies, middle-aged ones, or else growing up fast. Their life-span is so short that even the screen's more recent nymphets – Tatum O'Neal, Jodie Foster, Nastassia Kinski – are playing mature roles, if they are acting at all. A smattering of European 'nymphet' films have brought sudden stardom to girls like Sophie Marceau and Charlotte Gainsbourg in France and to Emily Lloyd in England. They are hotly pursued by Hollywood, which seems to have run out of credible nymphets, despite its claims to have the world's highest ratio per square mile of nubile blondes.

But no really good Hollywood archetype ever dies, or even fades away. The great movie nymphets are still there, waiting to leap out of cans and boxes at a moment's notice, and never more so than in the age of video, cable and satellite TV, and the art cinemas that thrive in every major city despite the crisis in the commercial cinema. Leaf through any TV programme or video display anywhere in this shrinking world of ours and you will turn them up: Shirley Temple in *The Little Colonel*, Judy Garland in *The Wizard of Oz*, Elizabeth Taylor in *National Velvet*, Carroll Baker in *Baby Doll*, Sue Lyon in *Lolita*, Hayley Mills in *In Search of Castaways*, Tatum O'Neal in *Paper Moon*, Jodie Foster in *Taxi Driver*, Brooke Shields in *Pretty Baby* or Nastassia Kinski in *Tess...* the virtuous nymphets and the sexually aware ones, the innocent and the sly, the fey and the sensuous, the babyish and the nearly grown-up, the talented and the less talented, the gorgeous and the almost plain: each of them facets of a myth which has its poetic and its ugly sides, but which, like all myths, taps the collective unconscious too deeply not to endure.